we wear the mask

we wear the

MASK

15 TRUE STORIES OF
PASSING IN AMERICA

Edited by

BRANDO SKYHORSE
and **LISA PAGE**

BEACON PRESS / BOSTON

BEACON PRESS
Boston, Massachusetts
www.beacon.org

Beacon Press books
are published under the auspices of
the Unitarian Universalist Association of Congregations.

Printed in the United States of America

20 19 18 17   8 7 6 5 4 3 2 1

This book is printed on acid-free paper that meets the uncoated paper
ANSI/NISO specifications for permanence as revised in 1992.

Text design and composition by Kim Arney

Some names and other identifying characteristics of people mentioned
in this work have been changed to protect their identities.

Library of Congress Cataloging-in-Publication Data
Names: Skyhorse, Brando, editor. | Page, Lisa Frazier, editor.
Title: We wear the mask : 15 true stories of passing in America /
edited by Brando Skyhorse & Lisa Page.
Description: Boston : Beacon Press, 2017. | Includes bibliographical references.
Identifiers: LCCN 2016058349 (print) | LCCN 2017014930 (ebook) | ISBN
9780807078990 (ebook) | ISBN 9780807078983 (pbk. : alk. paper)
Subjects: LCSH: Ethnicity—United States. | Passing (Identity)—United States.
Classification: LCC E184.A1 (ebook) | LCC E184.A1 W327 2017 (print) |
DDC 305.800973—dc23
LC record available at https://lccn.loc.gov/2016058349

We wear the mask that grins and lies,
It hides our cheeks and shades our eyes,—
This debt we pay to human guile;
With torn and bleeding hearts we smile,
And mouth with myriad subtleties.

Why should the world be over-wise,
In counting all our tears and sighs?
Nay, let them only see us, while

We wear the mask.
We smile, but, O great Christ, our cries
To thee from tortured souls arise.
We sing, but oh the clay is vile
Beneath our feet, and long the mile;
But let the world dream otherwise,
We wear the mask!

—PAUL LAURENCE DUNBAR

CONTENTS

EDITORS' NOTE

In June 2015 a surprising number of Americans stopped to gawk at a thirty-seven-year-old "African American" woman named Rachel Dolezal who, after an almost decade-long act, was outed by her parents as a white woman who chose to pass as black. The national response, culminating in a *Today* show appearance, was extreme. Some were outraged by her deception, while others drew parallels between her right to live her "truth" the same way Caitlyn Jenner embodies hers.

Rachel—or "#BlackRachel" as she trended online—never once "broke character."

Later that month, the *Daily Beast* reported on Andrea Smith, an Anglo woman and esteemed professor of Native American studies at the University of California, Riverside, who presented as Cherokee for over twenty years. She had a long history of American Indian activism and published articles and books purporting to speak on Indian issues *as an American Indian* despite not a trace of Indian ancestry being found after two rounds of genealogical research.

If you're looking for historical precedent, how about jazz clarinetist Mezz Mezzrow? A middle-class Jewish kid from Chicago, he married a black woman, moved to Harlem, self-identified in the 1940s as a "white Negro" and was listed by his draft board as "Negro." His understanding of being a black American was an odd brew of sincere cultural musical appreciation and promoting the oversimplified "shuck and jive" stereotypes. Go back further and you'll find Clarence King, a nineteenth-century blue-eyed white scientist and best-selling author who thrilled in "slumming." For thirteen years, King passed as a black Pullman porter, complete with a black common-law wife and five mixed-race children.

American history is filled with innumerable examples like these. Why, then, did "#BlackRachel" fascinate and outrage so many of us? The answer lies in the complex phenomenon of *passing*.

"Passing," as Brando Skyhorse notes in his essay, "is when someone tries to get something tangible to improve their daily quality of life by occupying a space meant for someone else."

Many Americans believe—or insist—our country operates on a color-blind system of meritocratic fairness. Others feel they've been victimized by a system that belittles or erases them. Passing is problematic because it's a hack on a racially biased societal construct that shouldn't exist. People who can pass are racial "one percenters," who by "cheating" the system win access to the specific life they want, the ultimate form of assimilation, the pure embodiment of the American Dream.

Why do people pass? The reasons are manifold: opportunity, access, safety, adventure, agency, fear, trauma, shame. Some pass to advance themselves or their loved ones to what they perceive is a better quality of life. Others are passed on by gatekeepers, who see in the person they're passing some kind of kinship, an element that says, "You're like me. And now, you belong."

Passing is an intensely personal issue for both editors of this book. One of us, Brando Skyhorse, is a Mexican American who passed as an American Indian for over twenty-five years. He passed as an Indian because his mother, Maria Teresa, who was afflicted with borderline personality disorder, asked him to.

Unlike Rachel and Andrea, who are white, his mother was a Mexican American woman who "reinvented" herself as an American Indian named Running Deer and lived that way for decades. He was her unknowing, and then, when he was old enough to understand the lie, willing accomplice in acting Indian.

Our other editor, Lisa Page, is a woman whose black great-grandmother passed for white in Mississippi, to get a college education. Lisa's white mother also passed, as a woman without biracial children. She was ashamed of her interracial marriage and hid her children's ethnicity during the last years of her life.

Each of the fifteen writers in this collection had to wrestle with serious questions in their own specific way: Have they passed as someone they were not? What was their agenda? What did they gain and lose from the experience? Were they worried about stoking feelings of resentment toward a specific community? Was it selfish pity by proxy? Were they mining the plight of other marginalized individuals or trying to rescue themselves from their own marginalized groups? How did each of these authors play on stereotypes (or sympathies) to pass? How did they feel about passing when they didn't intend to? Have they written about passing before and, if so, has their thinking about it evolved over time?

Our writers have been fearless on these pages in how they explored fluid identities, code switching, and assimilation. They share how passing transcends race, religion, ethnicity, and various kinds of orientation. Patrick Rosal, who writes about being mistaken for the help at the National Book Awards, asked if we had considered disability passing. Ashamed of his hearing impairment, Rosal realized he was pretending his tinnitus didn't exist and was passing as a man without hearing loss. Once you acknowledge how prevalent passing is, you're liable to spot variations of it everywhere.

Since the 2008 economic downturn, class passing is rampant. Gender and sexuality passing continues to evolve. Racial and ethnic passing is far more complicated than the old stories of crossing the color line for a job opportunity. Passing is a part of how many Americans survive, but it also brings inherent risks. One of our favorite lines from this collection is from Gabrielle Bellot: "Passing, like prettiness, is a privilege; passing, like prettiness, can also be a peril, if someone believes we are deceiving them." What we hope you'll realize from these essays is that, whether you've been conscious of it or not, passing is a privilege all of us have indulged in at some point. People make assumptions about us based on stereotypes, context, environment. When we don't correct these ideas, either because we genuinely like the assumptions someone's made about us, or because explaining the truth could humiliate, or infuriate, whoever's making these assumptions, we "pass." We misrepresent ourselves in classrooms or at airports, on Facebook and at dinner parties. Maybe we haven't reached Rachel Dolezal's level of racial performance, which incorporated hair weaves and skin tanners, but each of us sometimes employs misdirection to let someone jump to a different conclusion about who we are.

"Passing," Bellot observes, "is a thing with wings, fins, and ghost-light feet, a thing that follows me everywhere." When someone asks one of our contributors—and it is a question each one of us has been asked—"*What* are you?" or "*Who* are you?"—you'll see that "Who do you think I am?" isn't a defiant or glib retort. Read these essays, then ask yourself: *How would* I *answer?*

—B.S. & L.P.

College
Application Essay #2

/ Brando Skyhorse /

I was seventeen when I had to choose who I was going to be for the rest of my life. In late 1990 I applied for college as an American Indian named Brando Skyhorse, using the identity my mother created for me when I was three, after my Mexican biological father abandoned us. Born Maria Teresa, she abandoned her own Mexican identity at the same time and reinvented herself as Running Deer Skyhorse.

I'd known I was a Mexican named Brando Ulloa since I was about twelve or thirteen, but I lied on my applications because being an Indian was who my mother wanted me to be. She embraced her Indianness and expected me to do the same. My mother had borderline personality disorder and was not a woman you disagreed with.

To her, we weren't acting. We *were* American Indians.

I knew biologically I wasn't American Indian. But I wasn't sure I was Mexican, either. My mother was a fantastic liar who'd say my father was an American Indian on Tuesday, "maybe" a Mexican on Wednesday, and a "none of your goddamned business" every other day of the week. We were on stepfather number four in 1990 (there'd be five total) and even *he* didn't know we weren't American Indians. What basic understanding of Mexicanness I had was through my grandmother. She snuck in bits and pieces of Spanish and *cultura* in our daily conversations, as if she were hiding broccoli in a slice of *pastel de tres leches.* That's how I learned that *payaso* meant clown, as in, "Your stepfather's a drunken *payaso.*" That's how I learned about the Zoot Suit riots, Chavez Ravine, and the 1968 Chicano student walkouts in East LA. Her history—*our* history—stuck, but little else did. Our family didn't "present" ourselves in ways my Mexican friends did: Catholic church on Sunday, big family dinners at an ancient table instead of TV trays in front of separate TVs, celebrating Las Posadas at Christmas. I knew more words in what my mother told me was Apache than I did in Spanish.

On my college applications I wrote essays about living as an American Indian in Los Angeles—*As a Native American living in present-day society, I do not often fit what one person's idea of what an Indian should look like.* Some of this was true; I was a misfit in my neighborhood, struggling to dress as some kind of 1980s new-wave rock star. I matched baggy Cavariccis from Chess King with black short-sleeve Bugle Boy bowling shirts from Gerry's, the old man's clothing store down the block on Sunset. I could never get my face right, though. Eyeliner and bright red lipstick weren't a great match for brown skin.

Being Indian became an important point when I applied to top-tier schools. Several friends said that, regardless of my excellent grades and strong scores (even twenty-five years later I feel the need to validate my performance), my American Indian name would guarantee I'd rise to the top of the affirmative action pool. Of course, I'd have likely been evaluated a similar way had I applied with my Mexican American last name, Ulloa, or if I had been rich and used my family connections. My undergraduate adviser, who also didn't know I wasn't Indian, later confirmed, "Affirmative action, nepotism, money: it's all the same. Everyone uses whatever they have to get in."

I was accepted several places, including Dartmouth, which sent me round-trip tickets to visit the campus. Dartmouth's 1769 charter mandated a school "for the education and instruction of Youth of the Indian Tribes in this Land." This meant Dartmouth made recruiting American Indians an active priority. I didn't know this when I applied, but suspected, after three insistent phone calls, that the little race box I'd checked, and subsequently corroborated with stories I told in my college interview and my college essays, had been the deciding factor in my acceptance.

How could I take something that didn't belong to me? I stared at the dollar value of the plane tickets—over $1,000— and imagined that money in a sack with a dollar sign on it as something I'd swiped, and stalled about visiting the campus. My counselors and teachers didn't understand. Why decide before seeing the place for myself? Was it the distance, New Hampshire being so far from LA? Maybe I was afraid to fly?

None of the school adults knew I wasn't Indian. Some of my friends knew I was Mexican but didn't understand why I was conflicted. "You have an Indian name and an Indian stepdad. You're more Indian than anyone I've ever met."

Stepdad number four said, "Nobody gives us white men anything for just being white! Appreciate it!" (He'd skip town a month later, outrunning an embezzlement charge at the chain restaurant he managed.)

My Asian girlfriend said, "Just take the trip and see what it's like." She knew I was Mexican too because she'd dumped me six weeks into our relationship when I told her I wasn't Indian. "Chinese can't be with Mexicans. Whites are okay. Indians are

rare, so they don't count with my parents. Blacks and Mexicans—
uh-uh." In Echo Park, it felt natural for Mexicans and Asians to
distrust one another, not the economic system that made them
fight for the same immigrant table scraps.

We reconciled our breakup two days later. This was her at-
tempt to be supportive.

"Quit being so honest," my mother said. "Are you my son
or not? Nobody's as good as you're pretending to be. Take the
trip. Someone wants to give you something and you're making
them feel bad by refusing. Haven't I taught you anything about
white people?"

Given my family's subsistence on welfare and SSI, I would
have received a complete financial-aid package. For four years, I
wouldn't have any monetary need at Dartmouth College.

All I had to do was say yes.

I wrapped the tickets in several sheets of aluminum foil and,
early one morning, mailed them back without any accompanying
letter or explanation. Those tickets belonged to someone else.
Someone I knew I wasn't.

I couldn't admit to *everyone* I wasn't that person, though. I'd
applied as an American Indian to other schools, including Stanford, which is where I went instead. Unable to acknowledge I
was Mexican to everyone, I continued passing as an American Indian. It was a temporary hedge that was in actuality a worst-case
scenario. Being a Mexican became a guarded secret that I'd have
to twist and contort myself around. My lack of a birth certificate
or a Social Security card with my name on it meant I couldn't
get a driver's license or open a bank account to cash work or
financial-aid checks.

"Look in the backs of these," my mother said, and gave me
a stack of *Official Detective* true-crime magazines. "You can buy
fake IDs in any name you want."

My mother told me I was dumb for not taking the Dartmouth trip and I believed her. That decision led to me choosing a school much closer to her and her BPD-fueled abuse. In New Hampshire, I could have cut the dysfunctional tether that kept us together by telling her I couldn't afford to fly back over breaks throughout the year. Maybe I could have become who I wanted to be sooner, something that wasn't possible at a college just a seven-hour drive from Echo Park on a single highway.

It took me years before I forgave myself for telling the truth. Which is why I want to tell the truth now, about how I passed—and how people passed me off—as an American Indian. I hesitated to share what's here for years because I thought I'd be called a fraud, a thief, a liar, and given how often my mother and grandmother abused me, why give their voices any help?

In 2014, Bennington College, where I taught a course on passing, introduced a supplemental undergraduate application process called "dimensional admissions." The process lets students decide what an admissions committee will review in their application portfolio. "A successful Dimensional Application demonstrates," among other things, "a capacity to design an inquiry, create and revise work; a tolerance for ambiguity, self-direction, self-reflection, and self-restraint."

These qualities, essential for collegiate success, are also the survival skills I needed as a Mexican American, passing as an American Indian, to gradually accept who—and what—I really am.

IDENTIFYING PROSPECTS

"Passing" is when someone tries to get something tangible to improve their daily quality of life by occupying a space meant for someone else. How does passing work? You start by identifying the prospects. That is, what space do you have now, what space would it be preferable for you to occupy instead, and why?

I was three when my Mexican American mother, Maria Teresa, was abandoned by my Mexican biological father, Candido Ulloa. She had been about the same age when her Mexican father, Tomás, abandoned her. My mother grew up speaking basic Spanish but made no effort to learn more. Her childhood was no different than that of many Latino children whose parents want them to assimilate and know that the cost of being a "real" American is sacrificing as much of your identity and language as possible. The goal is to blend in, not to call attention to yourself, for a lot of reasons. You could arouse the suspicion of a police officer looking for random brown people to stop. You could draw the ire of an angry white person who imagines you've wronged them in some way and, if you're lucky, decides only to shout at you. "La Migra!" maybe, or "Go back to Mexico!" in a state that was once part of Mexico.

Maria was a wife without a husband, with a child who had no father. We were brown, poor, a pair of clichéd statistics. We were nothing.

If you're nothing, the goal is for you to become something. If that isn't possible—and she felt it wasn't for Mexicans in Los Angeles during the 1970s—the next step is to become someone else. My mother's skin was too dusky, her cheekbones too pointed, to pass as white. Who else, then?

From the late 1960s to the mid-1970s there was a heightened media awareness of Indian activism fueled in large part by the American Indian Movement. AIM led a series of high-profile "takeovers" in this period, of Alcatraz prison, the Bureau of Indian Affairs building in Washington, DC, and the town of Wounded Knee, South Dakota. At the 1973 Academy Awards, Marlon Brando sent the Native American activist Sacheen Littlefeather onstage in his place to refuse his Best Actor Oscar as a means of protesting Hollywood's denigration of American Indians and their culture.

Five months later, I was born Brando Ulloa. I might have stayed that way but, a year later, a cab driver was murdered at an Indian camp in Ventura, California. The suspects were Paul Skyhorse Durant, a twenty-nine-year-old Chippewa Indian, and Richard Mohawk. The Skyhorse/Mohawk trial—what a name for a political ticket!—dragged on for over three years before ending in acquittals and became LA's highest-profile murder case in the 1970s. During the trial, Candido left and my mother initiated a correspondence with Durant. He was married with children but her enclosed pictures earned her a spot on his visitors' list.

Stephen King says that a good story happens when "two previously unrelated ideas come together and make something new under the sun."

My mother wanted her own Paul Skyhorse. She wanted to *be* a Skyhorse too. That wasn't possible with Durant, so she corresponded via a classified singles ad with an American Indian inmate named Paul Martin Henry Johnson, incarcerated in Illinois for armed robbery. Over a period of several months and many exchanged letters, Paul Johnson emerged as "Paul Skyhorse Johnson." That was how he introduced himself when I met him inside a prison. *Paul Skyhorse Johnson. Your father.* I was five years old.

With Paul's Indianness, she had something she craved more than acceptance into a community. She had authenticity. She had a name.

Running Deer Skyhorse, a name she created, was Somebody. Brando Skyhorse, the son of an imprisoned American Indian chief, was Someone.

PERFORMANCE

Passing requires a knowing decision about hiding or omitting one's background to obtain acceptance into a community. This is performance.

There were three important aspects to our passing act. It was the 1980s, so, of course, hair was an important tool. Hair could make gawky suburban white boys into rock stars. It could also make ordinary Mexicans into fetishized American Indians.

Running Deer grew her hair midway to her waist, dying it an unnatural fire-truck red. It was a color also unnatural for American Indians. I'd go an entire school year without a haircut because long hair was "an important part of my heritage."

Second: props, an important part of my passing heritage. Running Deer bought me child's-size T-shirts with pictures of Geronimo and Crazy Horse on them, superimposed over slogans like FIRST COME, LAST SERVED. She prepped me on how to respond if any white administrators tried to make me change my clothes.

"Walk away. Run if you have to. Tell them I'll call your father who'll then call his AIM brothers. Don't let *any* motherfucker touch you."

My mother had several chests of southwestern jewelry bought from J. C. Penney and the Wild West Ghost Town section at Knott's Berry Farm. She'd walk into a jewelry store wearing a squash blossom necklace, rub turquoise pieces between her fingers, and proclaim to anyone in earshot that, just by touching them, she knew which had been made by an actual "skin" and which were fakes.

Last, language. "Skins" were Indians, "pilgrims" were white people, cops were "pigs," women were "squaws" (a word some Indians find offensive), and "apples" were Hollywood Indians who, while red on the outside, were "white" on the inside. It was one of her favorite words to insult me with. What did it matter if neither of us was red at all? We looked Indian, talked Indian, even listened to Indian music! My mother spun Redbone, Buffy Sainte-Marie, and, on repeat, XIT's *Plight of the Redman*, a 1972

Motown album that mixed "Native drumming and singing in the Navajo language"* with guitar rock and spoken word. Her favorite track, "End," has a spoken word speech by Mac Suazo. His voice, first as calm as a PBS narrator's, rises to a fiery crescendo. My mother stomped her feet in time with the drums and screamed Mac's lyrics every day like a call to prayer: *We must now manage our own affairs and control our own lives and through it all / Remain to be / The True American!*

Remember, we weren't playing Indians. We were playing *caricatures* of Indians. My mother passed as an Indian because, I think, she hated the idea of being no one, which to her meant being like *everyone* else in Echo Park. If I am generous, I want to believe she hated the thought that this would be my future too. She never worried about being found out, because she reasoned we were as close as most people would come to real Indians, anyway. She was right.

GATEKEEPING

A successful performance requires an engaged audience, or gatekeepers. These gatekeepers view either the passer's passive display (i.e., mistaken identity: *Boy, I could tell you're Indian by the way you stood there and didn't say anything!*) or active (modified behavior) display of a particular background.

My mother and I couldn't have passed without help. By that, I mean we couldn't have passed as American Indians without white people acknowledging us as American Indians. Our caricatures

---

* See Jan Johnson's great essay "'We'll Get There with Music': Sonic Literacies, Rhetorics of Alliance, and Decolonial Healing in Joy Harjo's *Winding Through the Milky Way*," in *Indigenous Pop: Native American Music from Jazz to Hip-Hop*, ed. Jeff Berglund, Jan Johnson, and Kimberli Lee (Tucson: University of Arizona Press, 2016).

were almost accepted at face value without any challenge. White people allowed us to pass—to become a "someone"—in our tacky costumes because the opportunity to say, "I met a real Indian today!" was irresistible to them. Our brown skin helped, I'm sure, but their story of meeting an Indian let them become someone too.

Passing usually requires acknowledgment from the group one wants to pass into—for instance, light-skinned African Americans successfully pass as white only when white gatekeepers mistake them for white—but there weren't (aren't) enough Indians around in Los Angeles to make this possible for us. While two of my five stepdads were Indian, you'd be astonished at how uninterested my mother was in meeting actual Indians elsewhere. She'd never gone to a regional powwow, visited an Indian reservation, or volunteered at the Indian Center in downtown Los Angeles. She'd read a few books, gone to a couple of museums, seen some PBS documentaries, but aside from pretending to be a paralegal assisting AIM in filing appeals for "railroaded brothers," there was little engagement.

Passing requires a decision about hiding or omitting one's background to obtain acceptance into a community. Community with Indians wasn't what she was after for herself or her son. Instead, community with white people was what interested her, what she excelled in, and what she trained me for, her "little big Indian chief."

Performance for white people equaled rewards for us.

GAIN

When someone successfully passes, they can occupy a new space in a "silent" or "loud" way. When biracial women passed as white during Jim Crow, or when, during World War II, thousands of Jews attempted to pass as French in Le Chambon-sur-Lignon with the help of its townspeople, their invisibility—their silence—protected them from prejudice, discrimination, and death. If someone passes loud (my mother, for example, and maybe Rachel Dolezal too), then the act of camouflage isn't survival, but a means to shed one's perceived invisibility, their *nonexistence*, so they can be seen, and their voice be heard.

Cul-de-sac conversations with white social workers, jewelry store salesmen—any conversation where some kind of transaction was required—blossomed into hour-long improv sessions once my mother revealed she and I were Indians. People didn't want to let her and her Indianness go.

How important was this ability in our day-to-day life? From the mid-1970s until the early 1980s, my mother and I traveled by bus, train, and plane to eleven different states. Five almost-legal marriages mean you have to meet a lot of potential suitors. My mother was a terrible planner, so each of these trips involved dramas, detours, late-night evacuations or early-morning cab rides through empty town centers or deserted Main Streets. Many times we escaped potential calamity or injury because someone made a split-second decision to help "an Indian mother and her child get back to the reservation."

Now, I'm not saying that we'd bilked trusting white people out of millions of dollars in a multistate, multidecade crime spree and buried our ill-gotten gains in a series of duffel bags in a cornfield. I never met a white person whose generosity couldn't be snapped back in your face, hard, if they felt you had somehow made them feel foolish, which is why my mother left places fast. It's also possible—in fact, probable—that had my mother relied on her charm, beauty, and vivacious attitude, instead of a stolen name and culture, we'd have gotten the same treatment and had the same experiences. In the moment, though, it did seem there wasn't a single interaction where we needed something, or something urgent, from someone that couldn't happen just a little bit easier once we became Indians to them.

Brando Skyhorse? That's beautiful.

I was far more visible as Brando Skyhorse than I'd have ever been as a Mexican boy named Ulloa. I hear from others how beautiful my name is at least once a day, every day. Today, it's hotel reservation agents, bank tellers, waiters swiping my credit card, but back then it was white women stroking my shoulder-length hair without permission and asking me questions like, "Do you miss your reservation?"

I could shrug offensive curiosity off with a smile. Kids were a tougher problem. They're better at spotting a con than adults are. To them, I was a sissy girl faggot calling attention to himself when he didn't have to. They somehow suspected, knew in their gut, my name was a way to get undeserved positive attention from grown-ups. It was a cheat, and kids hate cheaters.

LOSS

As Indians, we had stories. My mother took an incomplete assortment of modern American Indian history and put it in a blender with her own backstory. Running Deer had run guns—that's how she got her name—at Pine Ridge during the Wounded Knee '73 occupation by posing as a lawyer. She borrowed convicted murderer Leonard Peltier's narrative and upgraded Paul Skyhorse Johnson's actual crime of armed robbery, as if it needed upgrading, to double homicide of two FBI agents. Retaliation for an FBI shootout at his house, where his mother, Penny, was murdered on Mother's Day. I was the son not just of an Indian but of a chief, for god's sake! Of course, she had problems raising a chief's son. Like any spoiled, ungrateful child, I too was seduced by the white man's ways of Transformers and video games, but in a vision she had with a medicine man, he saw an eagle fly over my head three times.

"You will walk away from your people," she said earnestly. "Then you will return to the Indian people and help them. You will become who you are."

From Indians, we didn't hear stories at all. Stepfather number two, an Aleut Indian born on St. George Island, Alaska, moved into our house when I was nine. He was an inveterate con man and equal opportunity thief. Robert stole a van from the Indian Center and money out of my birthday cards and piggy bank. I asked him what it was like to be an Indian.

"I don't wanna talk about that," he said. "No Indian wants to talk about that. That's how you know you got a real Indian. Only Cherokees and white women wanna talk about being Indian."

Before stepfather number two even left, my mother had Paul Skyhorse Johnson queued up to move in with us when he was released from prison. Stepfather number two had a long criminal record, so she figured it was a safe bet he'd flee or get caught for new crimes before long. She was right; he fled about a year before Paul was released. My mother must have figured it was a good time to tell me the truth.

I was twelve or thirteen when, after bugging my mother for months, I learned my biological Indian "father" Paul Skyhorse Johnson was, in fact, stepfather number three. There wasn't a singular *aha!* moment, just a gradual acceptance of a different view, like a sunrise over a deep valley. It was a view deferred, though; when Paul moved in, he treated me as his biological son, and on nights my mother sent me out to retrieve him from a long, aching night at the bar, told me I was an Indian too.

"We're White Mountain Apaches," he'd slur. "The only tribe that *didn't* sign a peace treaty with the white man."

For my seventh-grade Young Authors' Project, he ghostwrote under my name an AIM manifesto called "The Shame of America." He had no problem with these inconsistent positions, so, my mother reasoned, why should I?

I had problems, though. Why were we doing this? Why couldn't I just be a Mexican? Was it that awful? I felt I was lying every day to everyone I met. I was a con man just like my stepfathers. No one understood. Not my best friend, a Mexican who, ironically, was a musical Anglophile whom I never heard speak Spanish, or my Asian girlfriend, who preferred my mother's fictional story of who we were.

By denying my authentic self I staggered into depression and came out holding a shitload of Depeche Mode, Cure, and Morrissey albums. Whatever empathetic gains my mother and I received from passing were emotional or psychological. Insignificant, or indiscernible, to a teenager, but don't underestimate how much currency that has in a lower-middle-class neighborhood to an adult. Indianness gratified and stoked my mother's extraordinary ego. That ego forgave her when her remedial Spanish stumbled out in Mexican restaurants in the white parts of town. She spoke Spanish the way a white actress pronounced the words in a Hollywood "Latin lover" romance movie. My mother sounded as if she was pretending to be Mexican. Not a surprise, since that's what she did during work hours too. For many years my mother was a phone-sex operator. Over several months she had a client who asked to speak to a Latina. So my mother, who identified as Indian to her coworkers and callers, pretended the part in a true *Victor/Victoria* deception. That is, my mother was a Latina, pretending to be an Indian, pretending to be a Latina.

It had a different effect on me. Whatever gains one is bequeathed or accepts from passing as a member of another group comes with a separation or disconnection from one's original identity or self. No small gain occurs in passing without a more substantial accompanying loss. I gained a fake American Indian identity, but I lost my actual Mexican American self.

In college, I hid from both the Chicano and American Indian student unions, unable—or maybe ashamed—to connect with either group. "We heard you were kind of a radical," a young Indian girl said to me in an outreach phone call freshman year. I told her I didn't let my race define me nor did I want to limit myself to "just meeting people like me." How radical was I to "stand up" to an Indian Stanford student who worked her ass off to become part of a student population whose percentages are displayed in decimal points?

I decided I wouldn't talk about race at all during and after college. During college was easy; in the early 1990s, nobody wanted to talk about race on my college campus. After college was tougher. I made this decision with a name like Brando Skyhorse and an appearance that's gotten me mistaken for Indian American, Sri Lankan, Afghani, and Turkish. It was not a very smart decision.

I didn't want to lie about who I was anymore, but I'd learn people wouldn't accept a simple one- or two-word answer about who I was, either. Not talking about race isn't an option any person of color in this country has ever had, in particular if it's not clear what race you are. If it's clear what race you are, you just get skipped an interrogation level. It's always your responsibility to address your race's stereotypes to ensure whoever's asking that you aren't like what they've heard. Be assured whatever they've heard is bad and you'll be asked to answer for it. Political correctness? Not in my reality. Political correctness never kept a racist from calling me a racist name. It's never kept anyone at a bar from dehumanizing me because I'm not their nostalgic ideal of an "American." It's never saved me from being reminded I'm an "Other." Political correctness isn't about depriving someone of their freedom. It's about giving someone the same inalienable rights that all "real Americans" have—the right to not be hassled, insulted, or assaulted because someone thinks they're different. In other words, it's about protecting an American's most cherished freedom: the right to be left alone.

Drink more than two beers in a bar and you'll hear PC sound its bugle retreat: *I don't mean to be racist, but . . .*

Here's how it works. I order a beer, start a tab. The bartender notices the name on the card. "Brando Skyhorse?" making my name a question. It's been a question my entire life.

I order a second beer. Bartender remembers my name, makes an innocuous comment. Buzzed single white guy at the bar strikes up a conversation. If I'm lucky, I get a one-sentence lead-in about sports or politics. Most times, though, it's a straight shot to Whitetopia.

"The government fucked you over, just like it's fucked me and every hardworking white man I know that can't get a job."

Mexicans, as it turns out, are dumb overbreeders who rape white women and their own bastard children, steal American jobs yet sap our vital resources through their excessive laziness and pot smoking, sneaking like rats into our country, onto land that was theirs as recently as 1848. Whites can refight a war that ended less than twenty years later, fly the Confederate flag, and call it pride and heritage. Mexicans are part of a massive Aztlan conspiracy to reconquer the Southwest, refighting the Mexican American War as lawbreaking illegals that should be sent home.

Then I spring the trap. "I'm Mexican," I say.

"I'm not talking about you, amigo! You, you're all right. I can talk to you."

That's what it's all about, really. Giving angry white men a safe space to be racist, where no one will call them racist.

That exchange is what happens on a good night. If it's unclear to someone what race I am, I'm treated to a series of interrogative questions, each more invasive, until it's clear what stereotype best suits them. Every month or so, when I don't immediately explain my name and reveal my ethnic background—the POC version of name, rank, serial number—I have some version of this conversation. Here's this month's latest variation:

"So, where are you from?" he asks.

"I live here in town."

"No, I mean, where are you from before here?"

"Vermont."

"*Vermont?* No, where are your parents from?"

"Los Angeles."

"I mean, before Los Angeles?"

"They always lived there."

"Why are you being so difficult? *What are you?!?*"

How I miss the gentle white touch of my long hair.

Continuing to pass as an Indian after college led to more absurd situations. In New York I was invited to a special publication dinner celebrating American Indian author Sherman Alexie. My well-intentioned boss sat me next to Sherman for no other apparent reason but, *Hey, let's sit the two Indians together!* Sherman asked me what my tribe was. I told him what tribe my Indian "father" told me *he* was, White Mountain Apache. Then a little joke to deflect from the conversation I didn't want to have. My mother, I told him, wanted to name me Pacino. (True!) Later, he signed a copy of his book to me "Pacino Alexie."

I stayed in the "passing closet." With each small step I'd tried to take revealing the truth, there was always someone there eager to help me back in. It was safer in there, and so much easier to relapse into a rehearsed story when everyone I met told me what I did wasn't even really lying. Why?

Take it easy, will ya? Besides, Mexicans are practically Indians anyway!

CONCILIATION/RECONCILIATION

Conciliation is one-sided. That is, a person who's passed from one group to another is comfortable with who they are. Reconciliation is the restoration of friendly relations with the community the passer originally left.

I've been "out" about being Mexican for about eight years. My Mexican unveiling and acceptance was a slow, gradual process. There wasn't a single moment, no simple update change on Facebook, no Aztlan eagle flying over my head three times. I still don't have a basic one- or two-word answer when someone asks me what I am. It just became easier to say in a rehearsed voice: "I'm a Mexican who has an American Indian last name."

Sometimes that leads to more questions. Should the Washington Redskins change their name? Sure—but *aha!* How can you tell them to change their name when you're guilty of the same cultural appropriation as Redskins team owner Dan Snyder?

What would you say to Donald Trump? *Adios, muchacho!* But *aha!* How can you stand up for "your people" when you're hiding behind an American Indian creation? Why not just change back to Ulloa? (Anyone who's been abandoned by their father knows better than to ask me this.)

A couple of years ago in Brooklyn, in a bar in gentrifying Bushwick, I ran into a group of young twentysomething white women dressed in faux Indian headdresses and face paint on Thanksgiving. A friend of mine from Atlanta was appalled and said, "You'd *never* see something like that in Georgia." I approached the woman with the tallest feathers and asked, "What tribe are you?"

She replied, "Cherokee."

"Oh, what part of the country are you from?"

"This is an art project," she said.

A friend of hers chipped in, "Why are you being so aggressive about this?"

I told them, "You're in a fake headdress and face paint on Thanksgiving. Do you wear blackface on Martin Luther King Day?" Pay no attention, of course, to the Mexican behind the Indian name.

I had a Facebook conversation with an American Indian PhD candidate at U of Chicago who friended me after my memoir published. Our discussion stemmed from Dartmouth's decision to appoint a self-described American Indian from the Delaware tribe to head its Native American Program. She wasn't Indian; her grandfather descended from Irish immigrants. The resultant attention led to her removal. What did I think about this?

I thought about a round-trip plane ticket to Dartmouth, wrapped in aluminum foil. I thought about flight, about entering a plane one person and in that flight becoming someone else, emerging on fresh New Hampshire snow as a confident Mexican, even at the risk of losing his scholarship because he was the wrong kind of person of color. And I thought about a Silly Symphony cartoon I saw many times as a child, *The Flying Mouse*. In it, a mouse saves a butterfly about to be eaten by a spider. The butterfly transforms into a spectacular Aryan blue fairy who grants the mouse a wish.

"I want to fly!" he says.

"A mouse was never meant to fly," she replies, but gives him a large pair of bat wings. The mouse flies over his brothers and mother who, spotting his batwing silhouette on the ground, race to their home inside a pumpkin. Running into a dark, sinister wood, the mouse meets a large bat.

"Hello there, brother!" the bat says and laughs. The black bat has large, bright, jaundiced eyes, stands twice the mouse's size, and flaps his wings like a vampire cape.

"I'm not your brother," he says, afraid. "I'm a mouse!"

"No mouse can fly," the bat says, and snaps one of his mouse-bat wings in the mouse's face. "So if you ain't a bat"—and here the bat laughs at the mouse—"you're nothin'."

The mouse cries, his lesson learned, and the fairy disappears his wings. "Be yourself," she says, "and life will smile on you."

But the bat and the fairy were wrong. The mouse wasn't a "nothing." His dream to fly *was* about him being himself.

Native appropriation is my mother's legacy to me and something I try to make sense of every day. You could say she was just another thief on a very long list of people who take without asking, appropriate without acknowledgment, and act as if good intentions supersede bad behavior. Or you could say that her dream *was* to be herself. I know she wanted to be Native, and when I confirmed her Mexican identity with friends and one of my stepfathers, they almost couldn't—wouldn't—accept that she wasn't. My mother thought belief trumped truth. She lived her life with a pair of bat wings only I could see. I'm sure she'd say it was the only honest way to live.

PEACE

Many years after my mother's death, I visited my first reservation, arranged by a nun I met during a Ucross Foundation writer's residency in Wyoming. I had Indian tacos on the Crow reservation in Montana, and then bought ceremonial sweetgrass at the Little Bighorn Battlefield Visitor Center gift store. There were many books about Indian history, and a video outlining Custer's Last Stand looped on a loud television. Every few minutes reenactment screams from Indian braves filled the store. Was this my mother's version of heaven?

Across the road from the store was an Indian memorial fire pit, used by Indian elders for religious ceremonies. My mother would have wanted me to burn the sweetgrass there. Instead I took it back to my writer's residency and, that night, threw it into an open fire pit. Under a bright starry black Wyoming sea of a sky, I breathed in the smell of burning sweetgrass and prayed to her idea of the Great Spirit. As a Mexican boy from Echo Park with an "Indian" name, I wanted to see my mother safely home.

William Faulkner wrote, "I am telling the same story over and over, which is myself and the world." Passing is both "myself" and "my world." This, at last, makes sense to me. Does it to you?

"Brando Skyhorse is a Hispanic Native American author."
—From the author's bio on Wikipedia

Secret Lives

/ Achy Obejas /

When I was younger, in my late teens and early adulthood, I used to play a game with myself called secret lives, in which I tried to guess how people imagined themselves. My family and I lived in northern Indiana, in Michigan City, a beautiful little beach town that depended heavily on Chicago tourism and the now-gone steel mills that used to dot the southernmost crescent of Lake Michigan. The town was majority-white, though there was a significant but mostly marginalized African American community. There was also a small but active Jewish community that operated under the umbrella of the progressive Reform temple in town. It wouldn't be until years after I'd moved away forever that Latinos began to accumulate and make their presence known.

Secret lives began because of my father, a light-skinned green-eyed Cuban who presented as a mildly oddball character. He was, for starters, exquisitely formal in the presence of Americans. He addressed almost everyone with an honorific and by last name; our neighbors of nearly thirty years were "Mr. and Mrs. McDaniel" up to the day my parents retired to Florida. Most days, my dad wore a suit. And on his head, a Basque beret.

Back then, my father did what so many newcomers to the US do: He reinvented himself. Not as a successful businessman or an American lawyer. What he created was a past life as an adventurer. At the dinner table, or during any of hundreds of drunken reveries, he'd recount long, convoluted stories casting himself as a champion. These were not tales in which the hero learned important lessons or conquered adversity. These were stories of the Cuban counterrevolution in which he was invariably the brains behind the operation, the guy with the steadiest hand, the best shot. (In one of his favorites, a friend breathlessly tells him, "Pepito Obejas, you have ice in your veins!")

Curiously, in our family, and in the family we'd created with other Cuban Americans scattered all over northern Indiana and Chicago, my dad was not alone. A lot of the men had wild, improbable stories: One uncle told some really memorable ones about living at the Brazilian Embassy in Havana for many months while waiting to get out of the country. There was also the gigolo uncle who'd married the well-off French woman (the only woman allowed in the men's poker game, I might add), and the uncle who had shot a soldier as they rowed away from the island, and the other uncle, the one who'd bested the commies with a casino scheme. (Don't ask for details—though these stories were often repeated, few made sense then and even fewer do now.)

Initially, my brother and I listened to our father's stories with innocent rapture. But as we grew older and watched him cower before anyone in a uniform or fret at the notion of completing a form incorrectly, we hurried him along, grunted at him. "We already heard that one, Papi," we'd say, rolling our eyes.

At some point, I'd decided these tales were Mittyesque fantasies with a Caribbean twist. Perhaps it was a condition resulting from exile; these men, after all, had left their home never to return and were struggling to find themselves in a new world they didn't completely understand. I figured these stories were the secret lives they desired, not reports from reality. Categorizing them this way allowed me to indulge them while keeping a safe distance from their outrageousness. None of my friends' fathers could match these tales, and I'd already intuited that the way my father portrayed himself in these exploits was unseemly by Midwestern standards.

Then, in my first or second year in college, I traveled to Washington, DC, as a delegate to the US Youth Council. William Colby, the former director of the CIA, was one of the speakers. I held him responsible for the assassination of Chile's Salvador Allende, whom I secretly admired (understandably, in a family of anti-Castro Cubans my admiration for Allende had nowhere to go but into my own secret life as a liberal American teenager). Some friends and I had determined to disrupt Colby's speech. But when we arrived in the hall, security was intimidating and we backed off.

Afterwards I stood in line to speak with Colby, still determined to say something in protest. Then the former CIA director looked at my name tag. "Obejas?" he asked. "Are you José's daughter?" All my leftie pals took a quick step back. It felt like I'd fallen under the hottest lamp in the world's largest interrogation room. I was stunned. Could any part of my father's stories possibly be true?

I was never able to solve the riddle presented by that incident, but it altered forever how I saw my father, especially in Michigan City. As he collected his apples (he loved apples) and fish into a grocery bag at Al's Foods and flirted harmlessly with the cashiers, I'd always wonder: Could any of them—PTA moms and 4-H sponsors, church ladies and Lions Club volunteers—see him as a CIA operative? Could they—*could I*—stand to acknowledge his secret life?

In Michigan City my dad was seen as a casual and harmless eccentric. His demons—his Third World soul, the ever-present wound of exile, the terrible burden of revolution and counter-revolution—were so well hidden, so masked by that beret and his charming Ricky Ricardo accent that had he ever mentioned his association with William Colby, I suspect no one would have taken him seriously. Perhaps he understood the risks that entailed, and that's why the stories were reserved just for us.

His tragedy was that no one ever saw the real him, no matter what he might have claimed. Had he ever chosen to unburden himself to one of those Al's cashiers, or to Mr. and Mrs. McDaniel, his stories would have been worrisome, not just because they imperiled his respectability, but because they brought with them a dark and violent world that my Michigan City neighbors—and to some degree me too—could only envision in fiction and the movies.

— — —

For the first three years we lived in Michigan City, we had an apartment right on the lake. My mom had chosen it because she liked to wake up and see the water: the placid blues, the stormy grays, even the endless white of winter. The neighborhood was, as we would say now, in transition.

For most of the calendar year, about a quarter to a third of the houses around us were empty, coming alive only when their Chicago owners returned for three months of summer leisure. The rest of the lakefront had a transient air to it: working-class whites who proudly displayed the Confederate flag (like the Marshall family across the street), young professionals just starting out (like the two bachelor teachers downstairs), young African American families (like the couple with twins around the corner), old Jewish landlords now retired who lingered all year long (like

Rose, our own landlord), and the rare stray foreigner (like us, except the others were almost all Eastern Europeans).

My mother's greatest hope was that we'd fit in, that we would be as much a part of the scenery as the sweeping dunes and the Confederate flag on the Marshalls' living room wall. We, of course, did not understand the meaning of the flag. Indeed, when the Marshall girl and my third-grade self would race up and down Lake Avenue on our bikes and she'd holler, "The South will rise again!" I'd join in. It was my father, having noticed the flag through the window one day, who suggested I should spend less time with the Marshalls. He explained about the Confederacy. "But we're not black," my mother pointed out. "It doesn't matter," he responded.

To her dying day, my mother would say she was white, never mind her nappy hair, never mind the map on her face that betrayed that assertion. I remember, at my dad's eightieth birthday party, my brother saying, "You know, if we are part black, we should be proud of our heritage," and my mother flinching. And then my aunt—my mother's sister—added, "Oh, if we are part black, it's so far back it doesn't even count anymore."

But my mother intuited something. Whenever she filled out forms that asked for a racial classification, she would fill in the box for white or Caucasian, then handwrite a parenthetical aside: *Cuban origin*. It would be easy to mistake that for pride, for a kind of patriotic assertion, but I've always suspected it was something else: in her heart of hearts, my mother knew her version of whiteness and the American version operated on very different frequencies. Her tragedy, of course, was the exact opposite of my father's: that she would be seen for who she really was.

But that my mother knew something did not prompt virtue. When I began working at the public library in my freshman year, I became friendly with my coworkers, including an African American girl about my age. Eventually we made plans to go to the movies. Too young to drive, I depended on my dad to get around if it wasn't bike weather. And though my dad hadn't blinked when I told him I needed a ride, my mom immediately interrogated me. As a teacher at one of two public high schools in town, my mother knew the girl and acknowledged she was a good kid. But she asked why, of all the people I could have become friends with at the library, did it have to be the black girl. None of my friends at school, she was certain, were friends with black kids, especially black kids from downtown or the west side, as was the case with this girl.

In the end, my mother ensured I didn't get a ride, and then foiled my few other attempts at this friendship. Of course, I couldn't explain my mother's objections—I was embarrassed, humiliated—especially because of her very public position in town, and my would-be friend naturally picked up enough racist vibes to pull away. My mother won that battle, and though I worked at the library for almost six months, I never socialized with anyone.

It's not that my parents didn't have friends of color: they did. Most were Cuban, or at least Latino. Meaning they had a shared understanding of color, at least in their own particular interactions, and everyone knew more or less where they stood. (Indeed, in this context, my mother was always white.)

Color in the US, on the other hand, was a mystery to them. When we arrived in Miami in 1963, segregation was in full bloom in the American South—a frightening situation they were unprepared for. I distinctly remember my mother pulling us away from drinking fountains and bathrooms, admonishing us to wait until we got home rather than contemplate which we might be allowed to use. These were not risks she was willing to take.

Indeed, in the only family story of racial confrontation, it's my father who's the protagonist; my mother is understood to be present, but she takes no action, has no opinion, merely follows my father. The story takes place in our first year in the US, in Florida, in what is now Kendall and was then long fields of tomatoes where my parents worked as farmhands. They had been hired along with a group of other newly arrived Cubans. When the food trucks rolled out at lunchtime, they were marked WHITES ONLY and COLORED. The Cubans—who clearly understood themselves as white—ambled up to the corresponding truck, where they were told that some, like my dad, could stay, but the others would have to go to the colored truck. My father, disgusted, responded that they were all Cubans, and they would all eat together, then promptly led the entire group over to the colored truck.

There are many things curious to me about this story. One is that while my father is identified as white enough to stay at the whites-only truck, no one is ever specifically fingered as too dark. I've often wondered if his actions were less a matter of national unity, much less racial sensitivity, than a question of saving face. Had my mother been singled out as not white enough? This would have prompted my father to want to protect her; it would have called forth his commitment to chivalry.

Another curiosity for me is that, though in this narrative my father acts heroically—precisely in the ways he tried to paint himself in the counterrevolutionary tales—he never told this story. I first heard it from my mother as an adult, in my late forties, after my father had passed away and my mother was feeling her own mortality. I remember one afternoon a decade later, after the birth of my son, when she and I were lying in her bed together when she repeated it. Then she told me she'd prayed and asked for forgiveness for all her prior racist thoughts and acts. It was such a startling, unexpected thing to say that we both lay there in silence and in tears.

— — —

Many years ago, long after I'd left Michigan City, I was invited to attend the Virginia Center for the Creative Arts. To get to this particular writers' colony, you have to pass through a tiny town dotted with what used to be called debutante colleges. Perhaps unsurprisingly, this town is also the home of Liberty University, the world's largest Christian college. Liberty's code of conduct forbids homosexuality; its founder, the late Jerry Falwell, once famously blamed 9/11, in part, on gay people.

I had no contact with Liberty students during my VCCA stay until the very last day, when I was accosted by a trio of them at the airport. They were fresh-faced and well scrubbed, and complying with the section of Liberty's Statement of Doctrine and Purpose that requires they spread the good word. For much of the time, I batted them away with a shake of the head and a few pleasantries. I'm the kind of queer who's usually identified as queer only by other queers, so I didn't feel especially targeted. But I still didn't want to engage with them—I had this distinct fear I might blurt out I'm actually one of those militant homosexuals they're always railing against, and I wasn't entirely sure of my safety.

So I did the next best thing. "Look, you're wasting your time," I told them. "I'm a Jew."

There was great irony in this—some obvious, of course. I mean, if I was in any danger as a lesbian, it seems obvious I'd probably be in danger as a Jew. But the greatest irony was not that, but that I should find any sense of comfort at all as a Jew. After all, five hundred years earlier, during the Spanish Inquisition, it was the very fact of Jewishness that had failed to protect some of my ancestors against Christian aggression, and given my family our legacy of diaspora and denial. The denial was so strong, our passing so effective for so many hundreds of years, that I'd grown up ignorant of my Jewish ancestry, something I only discovered as an adult.

It was at that airport that for the first time in my life I declared, "I'm a Jew."

And then I immediately looked around, worried that a real Jew might not appreciate my sudden affinity, might see it as flippant or merely convenient. After all, I have no Jewish baggage. I've never been bat mitzvahed; at that time, all my seders had been unity meals with black activists or surreal experiences with lesbian separatists who liked the twin themes of food and *Let my people go*. A real Jew might have seen my sudden claim as suspect.

So when and how do we belong? When are we real and when are we just pretending to be real? How fixed is the criteria that defines us? I have no doubt, for example, that my mother had African ancestors, but that never meant that, in Cuba, she was anything but white. I also have little doubt that my father's links to Africa were only primordial. In Cuba he was indisputably white. But here, in the US, he wasn't, even if no one ever told him to his face: his foreignness colored him and was part of what undermined his stories.

Now consider how wobbly my Jewishness is. To be a Jew, regardless of whether one practices, traditionally the main criterion has been to be born of a Jewish mother. That is not my case. But Reform Judaism and even certain Reconstructionist and Renewal congregations count patrilineal heritage so, as far as they're concerned, I'm in.

Am I more Jewish now than I was in that Virginia airport because these days I light candles on Friday night? Does the fact that occasionally we run out of Shabbat candles and use whatever's handy—say, a saint's candle more common in Cuban culture for santería—obliterate my Jewish intentions?

Jewishness is not the only aspect of my identity that's complicated in this way. I usually refer to myself as a Cuban writer, but most everyone else seems to call me Cuban American. And while no doubt the label applies—I was born in Cuba, I grew up in the

United States—among certain Cuban Americans I'm perceived as an American writer, because I write mostly in English. But if you look for my book in Cuba, it's not under the imprint for expats but under the domestic label, because sometimes I write in Spanish and because I do not advocate a policy of hate toward the island. My Cuban editor makes a big deal of reminding me my one Cuban book is on the Cubans in Cuba imprint, never mind that I'm not actually in Cuba myself much these days.

— — —

Years ago I had the rare experience of having my Cubanness blotted out for the first time in my life. In 2005 I had the privilege of serving as the Distinguished Visiting Writer in Residence at the University of Hawai'i—Hawai'i Nei, as my Hawaiian independentist students would prefer to say. And in Hawai'i, I didn't exist as Cuban or Latina, no matter how much I insisted.

The matter became clear to me when we did a group writing exercise in one of my classes that inadvertently produced a vicious and gratuitous anti-Muslim diatribe.

As a writer, as a writing teacher, I think everything, every topic, is game. In other words, if somebody wants to write from the point of view of a sympathetic Nazi, or if someone needs to exploit a particular stereotype—say, a pedophilic gay killer, in the manner of Dennis Cooper—I'm perfectly okay with it if it serves a greater purpose. I just want the story to move me, to illuminate, to disturb me, to take me someplace I haven't been before.

But this thing that happened in Hawai'i wasn't about that. So I decided we needed to explore the nature of stereotypes a little bit. Hawai'i is a funny place—it's probably the most racially and culturally diverse state in the US, but it is also a place where, paradoxically, precisely because of cultural imperatives against confrontation, the subject is pretty much *kapu*, as the Hawaiians say.

Part of the exercise I proposed involved listing nasty stereotypes about our own groups or demographic profiles.

To set the example, I started off, confessing my Cuban Americanness and explaining that in a US context we are often seen as intolerant right-wing demagogues. My students stared at me blankly.

I then said, Okay, well, we're also often perceived to be arrogant, anticommie capitalistic pigs. I got the same blank stares.

Getting desperate, I amplified my profile. Latinos, I said, are often viewed as illegal, uneducated, and clannish. Still nothing.

It's not that folks in Hawai'i don't know Latinos or that the islands don't have a Latino population. They do. But Latinos figure differently there. The Latino population is tiny, about 3 percent. And they fall into two groups, the conquerors and the conquered.

The conquerors were the Spanish and Portuguese, minor players in Hawai'i's imperial history who thus engender little attention or animosity and get kudos for bringing cowboy culture, the ukulele, and a pastry called the *malasada*. In the eyes of the Polynesians, the Spanish and Portuguese are foreigners, by default white. To use their term: *haole*.

The conquered are the Puerto Ricans, brought over at the end of the nineteenth century to work the sugarcane fields. Because they labored side by side with the Japanese, Chinese, and Polynesians, and because over generations their families have frequently integrated, Puerto Ricans in Hawai'i are perceived differently than on the US mainland. In Hawai'i they're frequently seen as modest, hardworking, and scrupulously honest. (Every Puerto Rican I've ever told this to immediately wants to move to Hawai'i.)

As a Cuban, I'm used to certain reactions to my ethnicity. In Mexico City and in Istanbul, when I say I'm Cuban, cab drivers ask me what I think of Fidel (it doesn't matter that he's gone:

Raúl Castro simply doesn't register). My answer can sometimes determine the fare.

But in Hawai'i, it didn't matter how much I raised the Cuban flag: No one asked what I thought of Fidel. No one asked if I lived here or there, because on the islands, "here" is Hawai'i, not the US, and "there" is the mainland, not Havana.

Failing to register anywhere, and looking white, I *was* white, a blank canvas to most folks in Hawai'i.

More than once I tried to explain where Cuba is, in the Caribbean, close, in fact, to Puerto Rico.

"So you're sorta Puerto Rican?" I was asked.

Resigned, I nodded. "Yeah, sorta Puerto Rican."

To this day, there are people I met in Hawai'i who have a special warmth for me because they identify me as something akin to Puerto Rican; that is, they locate their idea of who I am as a Cuban within their knowledge and expectation of Puerto Ricanness.

But here's the bottom line: in every single way, every day I was in Hawai'i, I knew I was Cuban, carried Cuba around like a scar. It was my vantage point and my curse. My inescapable condition. How could I live on an island and not view everything through my Cuban lens; how could I live on an island and not constantly contrast it and compare it with my island? How could I be white when everything about me was Cuban?

What hurt in Hawai'i was that even when I said I was Cuban, even when my companion had a sense of Cuba, it rarely mattered: "You don't look Cuban," they'd say. Or: "You don't sound Cuban." Or: "Cuban, huh? How about that . . ." My insistence on my Cubanness meant nothing because Cuba meant nothing. Passing as white and insisting on my otherness became my fate in Hawai'i.

— — —

Both of my parents were engaged in some sort of passing, with different degrees of fluidity and success. But for me, passing is effortless, and, frankly, not just in Hawai'i.

I walk to work and no one looks twice or thinks I'm out of place in my neighborhood. Sure, my usual turf is integrated, in POC-majority Oakland, California, but I could take the same stroll, with the same torn backpack, on almost any street in the United States and generate the same nonresponse. Indeed, when we visit my in-laws in overwhelmingly white Cedar Rapids, Iowa, I sometimes take solo walks and no one has ever been anything but pleasant. I'm not out of place; the assumption is that I belong.

The truth is, I can go into any 7-Eleven, Nordstrom, or Whole Foods, and I'll shop in peace. No one will tail me. No one will look askance when I ask, in perfectly crisp English, where I might find coriander seeds or the shoe department. I'm not suspect.

I register colorless, like most white people. The majority of the time, and especially now that I'm older, I'm marked sexually neutral, religiously unaffiliated.

And herein lies my tragedy, because while I'm fluent in passing, I'm haunted by the fact that, at the end of the day, I'm still this queer girl, this Jew, so very Cuban, if not on my skin, then certainly in my soul.

— — —

I know some things very well. I know I'm Cuban and, well, yes—American. I'm queer and Jewish. I know these things coexist and conflict and sometimes contradict. I chose my labels and sometimes, even against my will, the labels chose me. I identify and am identified.

And I also know that, though there are people in my family who are clearly of African descent, I'm not black, I'm not African, and that to claim that as an identity, as opposed to a heritage, would be false, misleading, and disrespectful of those who have really had a black life, a black experience.

My identity is fluid and incorporates my past as well as my new experiences. But I also know it is not infinite in its capacity, it cannot simply invent itself out of whole cloth. It is not a purely subjective experience. For example, I can't choose *not* to be Cuban, no matter what my citizenship papers say I am, or if I were to suddenly decide to change my name and live as white. The experience of being Cuban would haunt me, the way it haunted me in Hawai'i, because everyone thought I was white but I *knew* I was Cuban. Indeed, it marked and shaped my possibilities of whiteness.

— — —

Let me confess a few things: I have no ghetto stories to tell. In Michigan City, at least during my years there, the citizenry was looked at as black and white, without much concept of Latinas. I remember once, during a strange human relations exercise after Martin Luther King Jr.'s assassination, a counselor divided the class into two discussion groups, each according to her definition of race, and I belonged in neither. (Thanks to another girl in the class who didn't fit into the binary and who felt uncomfortable in the white group, we formed our own, a miscellaneous little twosome who made the counselor uncomfortable by defying her scheme.)

I've never been beaten up for being queer. I've been out for most of my adult life—a decision based on laziness more than politics (I simply didn't have the energy to keep the stories straight, no pun intended), and it's rarely been an issue.

Still, because my identities—plural—are not at all in the mainstream, managing them is constant, inspiring and illuminating but also exhausting and infuriating. Especially when it's not just about denying expectations and stereotypes, but also about insisting on identities that are often invisible to my interlocutors.

What to do, then? For those of us with multiple fluid or not easily located identities, our principal responsibility, I think, is to endure, to embrace our defiance of expectation, and to continue to tell the truth about our complex lives.

The Inscrutable
Alexander Fitten

/ *Marc Fitten* /

I.

My full legal name is Marc Jeffrie Fitten, but I have always disliked it. It's like the skin tag hanging from my neck that I keep promising myself I will do something about.

Since I was six, I have never been comfortable with hearing it spoken or saying it out loud. I have never identified with it. Ever since I was a child, everything in my DNA rejected this name. Probably because I instinctively knew it was a fake.

My real name is lost to my family and me. Lost for many reasons, but especially because along the way an ancestor realized his name gave away an ethnicity that was more trouble than it was worth. So he changed it. Twice. A shoemaker and a migrant who traveled around the Caribbean taking odd jobs, my half-Chinese great-grandfather managed to hide his identity from the people around him and from his descendants for one hundred years.

I imagine he did it to survive and gain advantages in life, but I believe his doing so left a family adrift—or at least it left me adrift.

Ultimately, Marc Jeffrie Fitten's identity has been as much a mystery to me as it has been to the people I interact with. On the surface, the name smacks of something practical and industrious—a midlevel bank clerk in a Dickens story—but really, it's a complete mess. It's misspelled, for starters. It also crams Latin, Germanic, and WASPy influences into a grab bag of realities wholly at odds with itself.

The etymologies of the names stumble over each other. First there is Marc—from the Latin, Marcus—derived from the Roman god of war, Mars. Then Jeffrie—a derivative of Jeffrey—a derivation of Geoffrey—which is Teutonic for "God's peace." Finally, there is Fitten—a derivative of an old Welsh name, Fitton. A Middle English word that literally means "lying."

Now, history tells me there was a Mary Fitton in Queen Elizabeth's court—that she may have been Shakespeare's "Dark Lady"—but this is only a coincidence. Wishful thinking. When I look in a mirror I don't see Queen Elizabeth's court staring back at me. I don't see the fall of Rome. I don't see a rising Germany. I don't see Europe at all.

When I look in a mirror I see a nut-brown face. I see slightly slanted eyes. I see thick, bushy hair. When I look in a mirror I catch a glimpse of the histories of many different peoples. All of them are more associated with the developing world than with high tea. All of them are more associated with labor and the capacity to endure than with playing lawn tennis in powdered wigs. It is exactly the way my face looks—the way my nostrils flare, my brow juts, and my eyes squint—that makes my name sound so absurd to me.

Throughout the majority of my youth, the inconsistency between my face and my name unsettled me so greatly that I endlessly questioned the reality of identity, race, and culture. I came to feel that these qualities were other people's projections of fantasy or fear. It never crossed my mind that a person could choose to be one thing or another, but rather that we are all a construct of mass psychosis, or at the very least, mass conditioning. This is a struggle I think every American deals with, but especially a person of color—wrestling who they think they are with who the world says they are. Dr. Frankenstein's monster and Shakespeare's Caliban are two characters that illustrate this struggle well. However, whereas those characters succumb to rage and desperation, my take on my own patchworked origins has always been a playful one—more akin to Woody Allen's Zelig.

I am a mixture of many different peoples and I have always enjoyed that fact. I am the mongrel white supremacists warned about. I am the Western world's bastard child. When I was young, I realized I was a fairly good mimic—I had a keen ear and could slip in and out of identities and across cultures. I became one of those annoying people who when addressed by someone with an accent tries to respond instantly with the very same accent. To this day, if I spend more than five minutes in any group I find myself mimicking the people in that group. The cadence of my voice changes. My vocabulary changes. My cultural references change. I code switch as needed. My need to mimic is so great and so unconscious that once when I visited my grandmother in a nursing home and she didn't recognize me, without thinking about it I introduced myself to her in a West Indian patois. We had a wonderful visit during which she kept asking if I knew her husband. My instinct is always to make others comfortable with me, and so I morph accordingly . . .

I suppose this is what happens when there is a family history of passing.

But then—and I can't stress enough how much this bothers me—I have to introduce myself as Marc Jeffrie Fitten and the whole charade falls apart. The name doesn't work.

I know I could change it. I know I could turn my back on it, but it has only been in the past few years that I started to have an inkling of what I might change it to. I am only just starting to know how to begin, and while that growing knowledge of where I come from satisfies my psyche, the problem I have now is that

I have too many options of names to choose from—more than I ever knew or could have imagined.

For instance, do I name myself after my maternal grandfather who hails from Michoacán, Mexico? Do I mix that with my original Chinese surname, if I can ever uncover it? What about my paternal Barbadian and Jamaican black ancestors? Do I find and choose one of their names to go by?

Would interactions really be easier for me if I introduced myself as Pablo Winston Chin?

They wouldn't. I don't think so. But they could certainly be more authentic.

The simple fact is, regardless of who people think they know in Marc Jeffrie Fitten, what they don't know is that for most of my life I have been a person without any family history—a person without context. My family history goes as far back as my family's arrival in the United States—all the way to 1950. Everything prior to that is tall tales and speculation. There are no photographs. There are no facts. Until I started looking, there were not even full names. Regarding my parentage there is nothing but the din of history and fabulist narratives told around holiday meals. It is as if my family materialized out of the ether and was just suddenly living in the boroughs of New York City.

So what came before? How did I get here? How did a decontextualized upbringing affect me?

Isolation, mostly. I had to spend the first half of my life building an identity from scratch—from the context of nothingness.

I understand now that I was a mimic because I was trying identities on. As there were no strings to tie me to anything, no ties to bind me to any tribe, I was free to choose. I was free to make it up.

A perfect example of this occurred in the seventh grade. Our class was given an assignment to bring in our family's coat of arms. I went home and asked my mother for ours. Her response was, "What's that?"

When I explained it, she went to a closet and pulled out a colorful piece of fabric intricately designed with geometric shapes.

"Take this *mola*. It's from the Kuna in San Blas," she said. "My grandfather was a full-blooded Guaymí Indian. When he got drunk he used to say he was related to Red Cloud."

I shook my head. It didn't make sense then, either.

"This isn't a coat of arms! It needs a shield. It needs knights. There aren't any knights on this." I was disappointed in her for trying to pass off a piece of fabric from her sewing closet as our family coat of arms. "It's just a weird-looking turtle. It's supposed to have knights."

"No knights," she argued.

"I don't think it'll work," I said. "I'm going to get a bad grade."

"Look, it's the only coat of arms you're getting. Just tell them your grandfather was an Indian. It's a totem."

What could I do? I handed it in. It never occurred to me to make one up. It never occurred to me that other kids in my class might have been making theirs up. In fact, it seemed perfectly reasonable that everyone in my class—all boys, all towheaded, all Christian—would have coats of arms. My teacher shook his head. He didn't like me too much to begin with.

"What is this?" he sighed.

"It's a *mola*." I parroted everything my mother said. "It's from Panama. It's our coat of arms. My great-grandfather was an Indian. It's a totem."

"Well, it's interesting, but it doesn't look anything like a coat of arms."

"Well, my mother said it's our coat of arms."

"Okay. Whatever."

It was 1985 or 1986. I suppose he knew enough not to fail me, but I didn't get an A, either. I watched jealously as the other boys oohed and aahed over their knights and dragons . . . and context.

I believe wholeheartedly that it was the fuzzy ambiguity of my early identity that drove me to become a writer and create contexts for a living. It is what drove me to build backstories and histories for characters I could control.

The need for context also spilled over into my personal life. By the time I was nineteen I had left the States and was living abroad—assimilating in Eastern Europe, of all places. I married a Hungarian woman precisely because her family hadn't left their town for hundreds of years, perhaps even a thousand! I found that level of investment in a place exotic and stabilizing. I settled roots down quickly—because I knew I needed to.

There was even a period during which I invented my own backstory. I invented an entire island nation for myself, Mondrovia—in the Indian Ocean. As a citizen of Mondrovia, I held long conversations about our Arabica coffee beans and famed miniature marsupials with countless waitresses, college admissions offices, and potential employers. People—who had never heard of Mondrovia before, or who pretended they had—were incredibly kind to me when they understood that I was a foreigner.

"What's your name?" they would ask—intrigued by the tale I would conjure up.

"Marc Fitten."

"Oh," they'd say, disappointed by the normalcy of it. Once, someone remarked, "Wow. There are no markers on that name at all."

"British colony," I said.

II.

The most context I can offer, regarding my history, is that Europe went on a five-hundred-year bender and needed someone to hold her hair back while she threw up. European history offers empires, expansions, and colonies. It offers revolutions, the Middle

Passage, the decimation of native tribes, and the Opium Wars. It does this from a thirty-thousand-foot view, listing the greatest battles and their generals, and keeping a tally of the gains and losses. What it doesn't do as effectively is consider the everyday lives of people affected. And the truth is, people had to react to all of that history somehow, and they did so through migration, miscegenation, passing to survive, and, finally, arriving on the shores of the United States of America.

An alien observer could easily glean the New World's greatest heroes. They could easily understand that throughout the Americas, men such as Columbus, Washington, and Bolívar are held in high esteem. Ponce de León has streets named after him. Even the two continents an observer would be able to piece together as having been named after the same explorer, Amerigo Vespucci. There is no shortage of statues of these men astride horses taming the land and hewing a new civilization out of the "wilderness."

But here's the thing—for every Washington and Bolívar astride a horse, there were an army of nameless people keeping their realities afloat. After all, someone needed to fix their shoes and watch their children. Someone needed to do their laundry. Someone needed to mend the sails, caulk the ships, grow the food, feed the other aristocrats, build the railroads, erect the towns, and carry supplies. This is just operational reality. This is the sort of messy back room that keeps civilization going. Washington and Bolívar didn't build it all with smiles and magic tricks. They had to work an army of others to do it. They had to break other men's backs to see it through.

That's where me and mine come in.

What I know for certain about who I am is that I am of the Americas and am subject to the history of British and Spanish empires long gone. I am a child of port towns and native women, spit forth from the sea, and a face like mine only exists because of the chain of events that occurred *after* Christopher Columbus stumbled upon the New World.

If the discovery of the New World had never happened, the English would still be English. An Ethiopian would still be Ethiopian. The Han Chinese would remain Han Chinese. But I, me, Marc Jeffrie Fitten, would not be here. And millions of *Americans* throughout the *Americas* would not be here either. We exist only because the New World happened. Our fates are intertwined. We are one and the same. We are a new type of person.

And this is heavy. The thought that so much history had to happen for me—and people like me—to be here. We carry the best and the worst of the old worlds inside us.

So though I might not know my parentage specifically, I have come to understand my global context. I benefit from my ancestors' capacity to have survived, endured, and adapted to everything that led to our contemporary world.

Here's what I know for certain.

In the late nineteenth century, in order to avoid being ostracized as an outsider who was taking opportunities away from a local population—and in order to fit in with a black majority on the British isle of Jamaica—my half-Chinese great-grandfather changed his name to the very Anglican sounding Aubrey Townsend. He married a mulatto woman, moved with her to Panama, and then changed his name again to Alexander Fitten.

Those are both dashing names, I have to admit. Aspirational Edwardian identities—perfect for people living in a colored caste system in a British colony.

The twist is intriguing as well. While mixed-race African Americans were passing as white in the United States, in the Caribbean, a Chinese Jamaican wanted to hide his name and ethnicity and for his children to pass as colored.

My great-grandfather—forever after known as Mr. Fitten—even had the good sense to die early, and so he took his secrets with him.

The most interesting thing about Mr. Fitten growing up was that he was a mythical character. His was almost a religious tale. For starters, nobody except for my grandfather and his siblings had actually met him, and they all seemed to hardly remember him. His death was horrific—he drowned in front of my grandfather on their way to deliver fruit to the United Fruit Company. Understandably, my grandfather never spoke of him. Nobody ever described him. His life was reduced to a few rumors and the capsizing of his overloaded canoe.

So the cornerstone of our family—and Mr. Fitten had two very large families who were a secret to one another until long after his death—was a cipher. He had two wives with something like twelve children between them. Not a single one of them remembered that he was Chinese. When he died, his children went on with their lives, their brown skin, and their Anglican name in Panama. He had managed to successfully hide his past and ethnicity, as well as that most basic element toward an identity—his surname. All fourteen of his immediate family members—not to mention their numerous descendants—lost all knowledge of and access to their original name.

I would call that successfully passing. And ultimately, that's what passing is: a person forging a new identity based on the fact that some identities have more unearned advantages than others, and the effects of that change on subsequent generations.

The tragedy for me in Mr. Fitten's decision is the implicit admission that nobody in the history of his family—my family—in the entire history of humanity, is worth remembering. That is a huge statement! What the passer is actually saying is that throughout ten thousand years of human civilization, several thousand years of Chinese culture, a migration across half of the world, there is nothing worth carrying. Alexander Fitten's original name didn't matter. It was just better to reinvent himself.

For a long time I couldn't decide if his choice was incredibly sad or incredibly hopeful.

We are all, of course, captains of our own destiny, and I would like to think that what he chose to do was brave. But his choice came with a price, and the price is simply decontextualization—abandonment in the cosmos, if you like. In the end, one man's choice is a great-grandson's existential dilemma.

Regardless of how I *feel*, the erasure is a powerful statement. Mr. Fitten didn't *have to* change his name; he *decided to*. He was not an African slave without a choice in the matter. Mr. Fitten's name did not have to be lost to history. He willingly gave it up on an island where it had been *taken* from so many others.

Why would a Chinese laborer make the choice to erase all the generations that came before him?

According to the tales surrounding him, besides the story of his death, there is the story of the land he owned and protected with dogs. Thinking this might be a clue, I hired a genealogist in Jamaica to see if there was any way to unravel his mystery. When I mentioned that he owned land, she said it was considered a sign of accomplishment.

This made me consider that maybe his name change worked in the end. Did Mr. Fitten only win these spoils after he changed his name? Had he sought advantages and opportunities beyond his station that only an Anglicized name could fulfill?

It raises more existential questions:

1. If a person has the chance to invent a more privileged identity for himself and his descendants, should he take it?
2. Is it a moral obligation to pursue these advantages for himself and his family?

3. If a social system is unjust and puts a certain type of person at a disadvantage, if they choose to pass are they disrupting and weakening the status quo or buying into it?
4. Should descendants respect this decision and keep the secret hidden or do they have the right to uncover the truth and claim an identity back?

While I can mull the first three questions over in my mind as much as I like, I never walked in his shoes, and I can't judge. I can only really answer the last one. Yes, it is my right to uncover any truth about my identity I can find. It is my right to hire a researcher if I need to, and to know what my name is and where it's from. It is my right to further the construction of my self-made identity with facts.

My great-grandfather—Alexander Fitten, aka Aubrey Townsend—changed his name and hid his Chinese ethnicity for three generations! The Fittens got whatever privileges could be had with their new name and the erasure of their Chinese ancestry. They migrated to Panama, where my grandfather went on to win the weekly lottery. He used the winnings to buy more land and ultimately migrate to the United States. Everyone in the family knew that their name had been changed, but they didn't realize that Mr. Fitten had a habit of changing names, and that the name they assumed was their original name was in fact just another false identity.

Being a Marc Jeffrie Townsend would be as ridiculous as being Marc Jeffrie Fitten.

The fable was fun, though. For the century it lasted, the family was comfortable enough with being Fitten, and Mr. Fitten could have gotten away with it for another century except for the context he left behind in his descendants' bloodstreams.

His genetics.

III.

In 2010—one hundred years after he had first changed his name to Aubrey Townsend—I received a frantic call from my sister. My two-year-old nephew had just been rushed to a children's hospital, where he was being admitted with symptoms that were alarming, painful, and potentially life threatening.

We did not know it at the time, but Mr. Fitten's manufactured identity was beginning to unravel.

Illnesses can be bacterial, viral, or genetic. Sometimes illnesses or infections can trigger genetic responses. As we know, Africans and African Americans are known to have a predisposition to sickle-cell anemia, while Ashkenazi Jews are at high risk for Tay-Sachs disease.

"I don't understand," my sister kept repeating. "They keep asking me if I'm Asian."

Asians, we eventually learned, are predisposed to a condition known as Kawasaki disease.

What happens with Kawasaki disease is that the body's immune system attacks the body itself. After a five-day fever, skin peels away from hands and feet. The lips, mouth, throat, and tongue become desiccated. They crack and bleed and also begin to peel away. The whites of the eyes turn red and swollen. Lymph nodes swell, and finally, if the illness goes untreated or if there are complications, the blood vessels in the heart or any other major artery can bulge and cause an aneurysm.

It is an ugly-looking condition; my nephew looked as if someone had poured boiling water over him. Whereas I had always rejected my name, this kid was literally rejecting himself, and it all pointed to the inscrutable Alexander Fitten.

I remembered something a cousin had told me days earlier. I hadn't responded to it at the time, but sitting there, I couldn't stop thinking about it.

"Your father took a DNA test," he'd said.

Until this moment in my life I believed that contexts were entirely speculative. At best, I thought, civilization was a hopeful hypothesis. At worst, it was an illusion. The only real things, as far as I could observe, were the precarious and existential crisis of the human condition, the capacity to love, the will to power, and the power of hope. We could call ourselves or be whatever we wanted.

Anything else, any political or economic system, any religious or tribal identity or affiliation, was a chimera. Bedtime stories for the feeble. As I had grown up without any real context, though it bothered me, I figured it was irrelevant. We are all, in the end, abstracted nonentities momentarily vibrating in the universe and trying to make the best of it.

That sentiment changed the moment I looked into the face of my sister's sick kid. *My* sick kid.

The bottom line for me now is, shit like this matters. It all matters.

In that moment, I realized it mattered that Mr. Fitten changed his name and didn't tell anybody. It mattered because in a split second it went from not mattering to being the only thing that did matter. Had we known the truth, the moment the doctor asked my sister if she was Asian, she could have at least said, "A little bit."

In that moment I understood that it is a simple truth that throughout our lives contexts exist outside our control that impact who we are. We walk with the past. Every choice our grandparents made has a bearing on us. I think that actively passing creates a context of absence—recognized or not—that can only be hurtful to anyone who follows.

So, no, the world does not always make sense, and that's fine too, but where it can, when it can, then it absolutely should.

And knowing who you are and where you're from is as good a place to start as any. It is, in fact, a fundamental requirement to moving forward.

So I called my father and asked him if he took a DNA test.

"No," he said.

"Did anybody come over and stick anything in your mouth or make you spit in a tube?"

He was quiet. "Is that what that was?"

"Yeah," I said. "Have you gotten anything back?"

"There's an envelope here."

"Can you open it and read it to me?"

He opened the letter he had received two weeks before my nephew was admitted to the hospital. It had account information for the online DNA service his sisters had set up. He gave me the information, and after my nephew was in the clear and I left the hospital, I logged on and read the test results.

Mr. Fitten's secret was completely exposed. I called my sister to tell her the good news.

"You're Chinese!" I said. "Enough, I guess, to catch Kawasaki disease. If they ask you again, now you can say yes. A little bit."

Honestly, she didn't really care. The strange thing about all of this is that I am the only person in my family this matters to.

I reject the name Marc Jeffrie Fitten because it is a lie and I know it's a lie. I am living a grandparent's lie.

And I don't want to do that. I have enough lies of my own I can sell myself. At the very least, I ought to have the stability of a name.

That is why I have taken my own DNA test. This is why I am still working with a genealogist—why I have paid a professional to search government documents, church records, and deeds and peel back all the misinformation. I want to claim this lost identity. I want to know all of it. I want to know because this is my life and it is the fertilizer on which my psychological development rests, and who knows? One day I might end up on a gurney myself and the knowledge of who I am or where I'm from might be the only thing that saves my life.

Even if I discover horrible things. Even if I uncover that my grandfathers were most likely European rapists or conquerors who took African and Native women as concubines, I want to know. Even if every encounter between my ancestors was a negotiated transaction, I want to know that too. And if I discover that all of my grandparents and great-grandparents loved each other and lived long happy lives together, then I want to know that as well.

It is the fundamental question we ask ourselves. *Who am I?* There are those who can never know. There are those for whom it doesn't matter. I am neither of these people. I do want to know. Furthermore, I have the power to try and find out. Only then can I change the question to *Now, what do I want to do?*

I may have great-grandchildren of my own someday. I think of it as a responsibility to them to break the cycle of absence for them. Some of them may be curious about these sorts of things. If that's the case, I want the ones who are—the ones who look—to know that they are not alone, and that they don't have to spend their youth wondering how they fit in.

At the very least, I can say to them, "Well, you are the story of America come to life. You can survive anything."

Letter to the Lady Who Mistook Me for the Help at the National Book Awards—or Some Meditations on Style

/ *Patrick Rosal* /

Dear Lady at Table 24,

    This two-piece fits me nice and slim. The jacket's athletic cut is tapered along the torso. The sleeves flash a bit of French cuff. Just snug in the shoulders with the lapels' gentle slope to the simple double button. Black, classy . . . and polyester.

    The suit is $90. OK, $105 after getting the pant legs hemmed. That's one decent night of drinks out in Manhattan or a take-home bottle of very fancy Italian red. It's a used TV. It's an Amtrak ticket round-trip from Philly to New York Penn. It's a used parlor guitar with a cracked tuning peg. It could buy me enough kush to get me lifted twice a week for three months.

    But I bought this suit right here to go cheer hard for some friends who are being celebrated at the National Book Awards. BLACK TIE, *the invite says. My seat at the table costs me almost two and a half times the price of my threads. I pay up because I want to be in the room to dap my brothers and sisters up. Get it?*

The crystal and silver is set over the clean white cloth. The hippest music is rocking Cipriani. Hundreds of glasses clink under the ceilings vaulted by these dramatic columns.

After the first round of drinks, after introductions and small talk with my table mates, after the courses of salad and soup, I stand up, excuse myself, and walk across the swanky hall, winding my way through the other big round tables to find my way toward one of my dear friends, who is among tonight's honorees. And you—sitting at a table not far from where my homeboy is sitting—stand up too.

Surely, by the way you crane your neck forward and to the side, stepping slightly left into my path just enough to intercept me, I must know you from somewhere else, right? I lift my chin a little to see if I can link a name to your face. And surely you think you know me too, don't you? I've traveled only from the other side of the room to walk toward you and for you to walk toward me. But doesn't something break just then, when you and I approach? All the festive shimmering in the space. These eyes. This face. I think I'm even smiling now, when you point back at your seat to tell me you need a clean linen to dab the corner of your mouth. You need a knife for the beef cheeks. A refill of your cabernet. Maybe you need me to kneel down and shim one of the table legs to keep it from bobbing.

So this is how you and I have been walking toward each other maybe this entire time.

When at first I don't respond, maybe you think it's too loud for me to hear you clearly. Or maybe you think my English isn't too good—for you ask me the same thing once more before you clip your request short and say: "You're one of the servers, right? . . . You're with the servers? . . ." And I stand there absolutely still so we might stare at each other for one long second exactly like that. "You're not with them?" You are pointing at the line of workers in white jackets and bow ties, a tray hoisted over some of their shoulders. That's

*when my face gets unfixed quick. I twist the whole thing—top right
eyebrow to bottom left lip. I crinkle the bridge of my nose and suck
my teeth once before I blow out a pfffffh! You open your mouth and
maybe if there were not the thousands around us chattering, prick-
ing each other with their literary wit, the fine chime of restaurant
china like a four-hour avalanche of muted porcelain, I think I
might hear you whisper, "Oh . . ." You spin on one heel and dash
back to your chair.*

— — —

I want to show you this photo of an old man walking out of a
building into the street with his hands full. He seems to lean to
his right-hand side, which holds the bigger piece of luggage. In
his left hand he holds a slightly more compact suitcase whose
handle he hooks with his three smallest fingers so his thumb
and forefinger can pinch some kind of stick—a broom maybe or
baston. I love his bright panama hat with its clean flat brim and
dark band. His pants are black, with a straight crease pressed
down the front. Even with one foot forward, the hem doesn't
ride too high.

For this man, it is still 1977. Not a week before this picture
was taken, officers of the City of San Francisco broke down
the doors of Manilatown's International Hotel in the middle of
the night with a battering ram, then woke this old-timer and the
forty other residents on order of eviction, despite a decade of
negotiations, resistance, marches, actions, and protests by thousands of folks from all around the Bay. The I Hotel residents
were mostly Asians, most of them *manongs*, a term of respect
for Filipino laborers who worked in America's canneries, fields,
and boats . . . They were poor, working-class folks and this was
their home since the 1920s, the one place they could afford.
Four days after the midnight raid and eviction, the manongs

were allowed to go back and retrieve their belongings—like this gentleman in the photo—though their units had been ransacked and vandalized.

Look again at the picture, the high shine of his shoes' leather. There's something so familiar about this man. Too easy to say he could be uncle or cousin. One of my dad's poker buddies in the '70s. When I look carefully at the man's attire, I think of the wish that attire can make.

— — —

Dear Miss Lady at Fancy Table 24,

You know when some third-grade kid is giving his mom grief in a store, hanging all his weight from the strap of her handbag or hiding behind the curtains or climbing into the metal shelves to lie down? Yeah, that was me.

Once every couple months my mom dragged me to the Rag Shop, a fabric store on Route 18, just south of the entrance to Exit 9 on the Jersey Turnpike. The store was housed in a huge space with giant windows and so much light it made me want to puke. It was always so quiet. I don't ever remember other customers in there, as if my mom was the store's only patron. With no one home to keep me from setting fires or flinging steak knives at walls or passersby, my mother coaxed me into the car and had me tag along.

I was bored as soon as I stepped in. I remember the tables and tables of damask and trefoil, houndstooth and herringbone, floral and geometric, madras and lattice and paisley. (I once found the whitest, most expensive bolt and ran my grimy hands and fore-arms all over it, and even wiped my cheek still greasy from fast-food fries.) My mother would spend my precious child-time sliding her palm slow under one sheet and holding another against the light. She'd touch with her knuckles and pull the samples close to her nose, examining the fibers. She'd select this one and that one, yards and yards, heaping them on the counter beside the register, and then she'd haggle like hell, pick up her several bulging bags, and turn toward the door, smiling like she just robbed the place untouched.

— — —

My Dearest Lady of Table 24,

Let's call what happens between us the Mistake.

The Mistake has billions of instances and archetypes and varia-tions. I think of it as godfather to the All-Black-People-Look-Alike Mistake and the Brazilians-Speak-Spanish Mistake and the Let-Me-Just-Say-Konichiwa-to-Korean-or-Chinese-People Mistake. And maybe the Mistake you made was the He's-Got-to-Be-the-Help-Because-He's-Brown Mistake.

I'm supposed to believe this fresh, albeit inexpensive, suit is the Real Mistake. I'm supposed to believe I'll never get away with this budget single-breasted outfit at a high-class soiree. Just a few weeks before awards night, I was striding down Bergenline Ave. in Union City when I passed this sale window teeming with cheap leather and zigzag sweaters, and I felt this little tug, this small yearning to slip into some fresh new fits with just barely wild lines, a chance to flip the fashion script and outdress the high-class gents who'd be in attendance at our shared shindig. It would just take a little frugal craft to make formal evening wear out of a simple but slick black suit bought from a dusty shop in northern New Jersey. And should I not have fallen a little in love with the gypsy woman from Valencia with a voice of straight whiskey whose sales pitch I bought in that province's Castilian? Didn't I drape that plastic bag over my shoulder already feeling the swagger of my get-up so hard that I left the store gliding out onto the public walk and then stepped aside without breaking stride to make way for the elder women of the avenue? Did they not acknowledge my chivalry? Did they not grace me with their affections by calling me caballero? Gracias, caballero!

I confess I didn't give enough of a damn about the cheap synthetic reek, the whiff of it rising around me as I passed among the gabardine, barathea, pure silk.

— — —

Dear Miss Lady,

I grew up around the corner from the old Fedders factory and the Revlon warehouse and the Ford auto plant (which is now a series of strip malls along a six-lane stretch of US 1). When I was in grammar school, the other kids at St. Francis of Assisi came back from Christmas break with brand-new ski-lift tags still attached to their zippers. They carved the slopes with new gear at Shawnee and in Vermont while my parents took me and my brothers to visit Uncle Ernie and Tita Candi over at Hoyt-Schermerhorn across from Brooklyn's Central Booking. Sometimes my parents missed the monthly on the piano in our living room. Sometimes Ma Bell cut our phone line for a while. Sometimes my mom had to rush a check so we could get the electricity turned back on. If you flipped the light in the kitchen late at night the roaches would scatter.

— — —

It was my mother who taught me to sew. I'd grown into a wiry, restless teen. It was the early 1980s, a brief few years when punk rock kids, b-boys, new wave freaks, and disco fiends might all get down on the same dance floor: this one in moccasin boots, this one in a track suit with three side-stripes down the sleeves and legs, this one in a baggy neon sweater and extra eyeliner.

I got just enough instruction from my mom that I could buy an eight-buck pair of black pants three sizes too big and hem the bottoms and taper the inseam so the ankle just barely let my skinny foot squeeze through.

I even learned to finesse the thread through a bobbin and control the fabric through her machine. I remember the music of her Singer. As a smaller boy, I used to sit underneath the table and slap rhythms on my lap or the concrete basement floor, keeping time with the motor's falling and rising whine. Sometimes it held a steady tenor ostinato moan and I'd hum in unison or sing some rough harmony a major-third above. I loved how her heavy scissors grunted like a pig against the old oak dining table that my dad stained too dark and which she converted to a space to sketch and tuck, measure and fold, stitch and seam.

Yeah, it was my mom who showed me how to select the needle from her tomato, snip the bit of string, and find the eye.

— — —

Dear Lady,

I got a couple college degrees. I'm a writer. I've published a good bit. I'm a professor. I have an office, tiny as it is. My checking account has been overdrawn four times in the last six weeks. My bank stung me at $34 a pop. Throw that on top of almost six figures in debt; I don't even own my sheepskin. My last dentist installed a crown to fix my back-left bottom molar, but the post shifted and cracked the root, so I'm doing it again after a new doc yanks the old tooth for another three grand. I've moved six times in four years. And now my landlord is selling this house whose third floor I rent. This summer I might be moving again.

— — —

Dear Lady at Table 24,

I keep thinking about those manongs of the I Hotel, kicked out in the middle of the night, the police and deputies barging through the double doors with a steel trunk. Cops in riot gear spill in from the street to clear the old men from their homes, some of them residents for half the twentieth century. There is footage of those manongs gathered in the barbershop downstairs, the diner, the pool hall. This one is slender, this one has a paunch. They are slightly grumpy and

*all beautiful. Woven into their manner is both gravity and play—
an affect you might get real good at answering to minor tyrants for
the ten or fourteen hours you work under the surveillance of some
other underpaid grunt.*

*I can imagine the body at work in the field. I can imagine that
body up to work before the sun's risen. I've watched my uncles and
aunts in their own fields of peanuts and corn and sugarcane. I can
imagine men on their various long roads home. Right now, I can
imagine one man pushing a narrow wood door that opens onto his
small room with a small bed and a good-enough window. At this
hour, he probably stinks pretty bad. He's probably sore and a little
stiff in his back or the fat muscle of his left hand. He might rinse his
face and scrub his armpits twice. The clear water in the basin will
cloud with dirt, salt, maybe a touch of blood from a cut in the thumb
reopened. The whole washing of the body—ass crack and groin to the
creases between the toes until he is renewed by talc and the musk of
his own long skin's oils. The man comes clean.*

*Maybe he's already begun to hum to himself. Maybe he gets
lyrics to the American standard wrong. He's not even smiling to
himself yet. But the music's already just under the tongue. He's
already forgotten the stupid shit the foreman or field manager
shouted down to him and his buddies. I don't have to wonder
too hard what men like this do with the first forbidden twitch to
strangle an overseer. How that wince is held back, pulled in. How
the whole arc of his fist, the turn of the hips, the shoulder's quick
pump, time and time again are stored away, like a journal for
the working body, a vocabulary one might keep, a babble, a violence, a nonsense, a bestiary of brutal motion, each figure honed
into a slight bow of the head, a loosening of the fingers to the first
knuckle, how one might peek through the top of his eyes so as not to
look directly upon a boss who is gazing back.*

*Can you see the body getting older? Can you see the unburden-
ing? The sloughing off of the more dangerous self? Can you see the*

man slip each leg into his boxers and a clean white T-shirt? At this
hour, in this light, the cotton's coolness softens him.

— — —

Dear Lady at Table 24,
    I confess I have loved you a very long time. And often more
carefully than I have loved myself.
    I see you. Dear Other,
    Dear Faraway,
    Dear Come-close-now,
    A style is not a category or season. It is not a box or bracelet or
coat. It's not a dance or strut. Style is a perplexity. A becoming.

— — —

My aunt picked the dress my mother was buried in. I can't remember it exactly, but the material was light, maybe had em-
broidery. I can't recall if it was something my mom made herself.
I hope it was. I'd love to know she could brag a bunch in the
afterlife.

— — —

I'm holding my arms up straight and sliding the silky black over
my shoulders and guiding my hands through the short sleeves.
I'm twisting the waist so the neckline's centered. I'm putting
on your slender dress. I have already stepped one clumsy foot
at a time into the panties, found the bra's clasp and clicked it
into place, tugged it twice to cradle my sad man tits. Now I'm
feeling for the single hole in each lobe to guide the diamond's
post through my ear and into the backing—first the left, then the
right. I still can't change this face, so I'll gently point my foot
over the arch and into the high heels' open toe. First the right,
then the left. I love the short swift current, these little gasps the
fabric makes around my thighs even in small turns. Now I'm

admiring my knees, my calf. Now I'm bending down to buckle the gentle ankle strap. I don't know how I'll climb out of the cab with any grace or make the modest ascent of stairs, let alone dance my ass off at the after-party. Am I a woman? A millionaire? A peasant? A thief?

— — —

Dear _____,

The word style *is cousin to* stylus. *It comes from the Latin "to etch." Or "to engrave." And so, style is a way to inscribe oneself upon the world, but also a way to dig, to delve into, to investigate. Style is, then, an inquiry. Style, furthermore, because it is a way to engrave, is also a way to carve a place into some landscape, a hole. That is, style is a way to prepare the earth for the body.*

There were early mornings, before my mom left for her job, when she stood in her housedress as she pored over all this fabric pinned to translucent tan sheets. They seemed an elaborate secret code, the dashes marking the cuts and seams, minor prophecies of the limbs' movements, articulations of the shoulders and hips, maps of an outer body and maybe even its inner space. The cotton sheets would run along the plate's feed dogs guided by her fingertips; she'd thumb a switch then ease her foot into the pedal like a rocket pilot. She'd hold the material flat, easing it through at gentle angles. In less than an hour she'd bite the last thread free of the machine with her bare teeth. And she'd have crafted a brand-new skirt or blouse for work in time to shower, pat her waist once in front of the mirror, jump in the car and go.

— — —

Dear _____,

One who slips on a fine set of threads does not become rich or worthy. He doesn't become boss or white or soldier or stallion. Instead, she enlists the outer rituals of work: the undressing, the washing, the slow dressing again into sleeker yarns. A way to touch and be touched. A way to see one's self before being seen. In the Mistake, one becomes nothing but a certainty. In true style, *one becomes a question. It allows us to hold for a while the possibility of fascination and the preface for awe. Only when style frees us into its peculiarities, confusions, or bewilderment does it ready us for the strangeness of living and maybe even a few humble kinds of love.*

Passing

/ *Teresa Wiltz* /

S o. To be clear, I am brown. That's not a description with which my mom would agree. "I never thought of you as brown," she once told me. "I just thought you had good color."

As she describes me in my baby book, I am, in the parlance of her day, "medium tan." Tan as in "tall, tan, and terrific," like the dancers had to be at the Cotton Club. Lena Horne "Egyptian Tan." Which is to say brown, but not too brown, a honey hue bumping up against the edges of the paper-bag test. Light brown, light enough to be accepted in certain social sets, but not super yellow. Not beige, like my mother.

I was born in the same week as Barack Obama, at the tail end of the baby boom, a tyke oblivious to the swirl of the '60s. And had we stayed in Washington, DC, the city of my birth, or moved down to Atlanta, from where my mom hailed, or to New Orleans, my dad's hometown, I would've been just light-skinned. Black, but "light-skinned-ed." Subject to taunts of you-think-you're-cute-cuz-you're-light-you-high-yella-bitch, perhaps, but place-able. Identifiable.

In the South, home of the one-drop rule, if there were hints that you'd been touched by the tar brush, even if just one of your many distant ancestors hailed from the Dark Continent, then you were black. Blackety black black black. White folks didn't want you. But black folks almost always claimed you—because what black family tree didn't have the stray white slave owner/overseer hiding in the branches?

Mind you, this didn't make you immune from the vagaries of skin-color politics in the black community. But it did make you clearly and unequivocally black. The lines were sharply drawn, even if you were Walter White black: *Go directly to the back of the bus.*

So, had we stayed in DC or moved to Atlanta or New Orleans, I would have grown up surrounded by folks who understood that being black was a complicated—and multicolored—thing. Instead, we moved to New York City. But not to Harlem. Not to Brooklyn. Not even to the Bronx—or Queens. We moved to Staten Island. Pre Wu-Tang Clan Staten Island. *Italian* Staten Island, circa 1968, where the "Tarantella" was the national anthem and all the moms but mine dyed their hair blue-black, teasing it until it stood out from their heads in massive bubbles held together by hairspray and hope.

There, the color line got awfully confusing for me. For a working-class borough filled with newer immigrants, whiteness was something to cling to. And cling they did. There were precious few black folks on Staten Island, and the other black families that I saw there didn't look like anyone in my family. Adding to my bewilderment: there were white folks darker than my mother, who was then—and remains today—unequivocally and unapologetically black.

Right after we moved there, the racial confusion set in for me.

White kids asked me all the time if my mother was white. The babysitter assumed we were all, from my dad on down, South Asian. In the playground, a blond-haired, blue-eyed girl shoved me and called me "spic."

We saw ourselves as black. The folks in our new hometown, many of whom were first- and second-generation immigrants, saw our family as something else. Different. Not black, not white, but something in between. Not easy to place. Hard to identify.

So, slowly, without ever meaning to, I started passing for Puerto Rican.

I was seven.

— — —

Staten Island.

Because my father had just graduated from medical school.

Because he was matched for a surgical residency at a massive public health hospital there.

Because New York always beckoned, and if not Manhattan, why not Staten Island, just a ferry ride away?

My parents met in Manhattan in the late '50s, when they were in grad school, two black doctors' kids playing at being beatniks. My mother studied French lit at Columbia, on the PhD track with fantasies of being an interpreter for the UN. But then she married my dad, and then he got into med school at Howard, and then she followed him down to DC, and then she had me, and she packed those dreams away. Because that is what one did.

In DC, for most of my early childhood, I lived with my parents and baby sister, Phyllis, in an apartment filled with midcentury-mod furniture. Across the hall, my dad's youngest brother, Charles, a dental student at Howard, lived with his family. And upstairs, another one of my dad's brothers, Fritz, also a dental student, lived with *his* family. My earliest memories are of endless parties and late nights and of cousins and aunts and uncles flowing in and out of our home. Of taking baths with my cousins and building fat snowmen that our mean landlady always kicked over. Yes, my parents fought, often bitterly, a foreshadowing of things to come. But mainly what I remember most about our little family compound was the love. And how everyone looked like some variation of me, from light and damn near white, to tan, to bronze.

Looking back at those early days, I can see how lucky I was, to have had that gift of family and connection and belonging.

I wouldn't feel that way again for a long time.

One uncle graduated from dental school; the other dropped out. My dad graduated from medical school. Everyone scattered, taking their families with them, one uncle to Los Angeles, another to Chicago, my dad back to New York.

To Staten Island.

The day Pops got accepted into the orthopedic-surgery program at the Public Health Service Hospital there, he and Mom whooped and hugged like they'd won the lottery. Finally. They were heading back to New York.

It was the beginning of a somewhat peripatetic childhood: we zigged and zagged from DC to New York, popping back to DC for visits. Ultimately, when I was twelve, we landed in Atlanta, where my folks settled for good.

But it was New York—Staten Island—that formed me, cementing my sense of self as the perpetual outsider. The universal Other.

Staten Island was a distinctly different animal from Manhattan, where my parents had lived as newlyweds in a sprawling apartment at 150th and Riverside Drive, for which they paid $150 a month in rent and threw parties overflowing with gin and cigarettes.

In that New York, Pops would haunt the Vanguard, queuing up to see Miles Davis over and over and over again. And in that New York, Mom hung out with a white ANC member, a woman who introduced her to the music of Miriam Makeba and to the frightening realities of apartheid. (When my mom's friend went back to South Africa, she was disappeared. Mom never heard from her friend again.)

Staten Island wasn't about the Vanguard and Miriam Makeba and white radicals from the Motherland.

Staten Island was a different kind of New York.

It was Fort Wadsworth, a military installation right on the New York Bay, where we grocery-shopped at the PX and saw movies on Friday night. It was both gritty city and isolated suburb. It was nuns and Mafia bosses, spaghetti and red, white, and green Italian ices on a long, hot day. It was swimming pools and hopscotch, playgrounds and jump rope. (But not double Dutch. Never double Dutch. Double Dutch was way too black for Staten Island.)

It was—is—Manhattan's far less tolerant cousin.

Of course, it wasn't like the South, where segregation was codified into the local DNA and Jim Crow made sure everyone knew their place. But that didn't stop the good people of Staten Island from burning crosses every now and then.

Just in case somebody got the wrong idea.

We moved there the summer of '68, the summer I turned seven. Earlier that spring, Martin Luther King Jr. was assassinated and DC, black DC, went up in flames. I stayed up late with my parents, watching the action on our small black-and-white TV, trying to figure out what the hell was going on. A looter dashed through my backyard and into neighboring Rock Creek Park, clutching an armload full of clothes. In the days to come, the National Guard rumbled through the streets in military trucks, while on the news, clips of King's speeches ran in an endless loop.

Such was my introduction to the civil rights movement.

The grief among all the adults in my family was palpable. I tried to understand, peppering my parents with questions: Why is he dead? How can he be dead and be on TV too? Why is that guy running through our backyard? My mother tried to explain the man and the movement: people were rioting because they'd lost something that they cared very deeply about.

A layer of sadness hovered over my city. And then, a couple of months later, as DC started to recover, we moved away.

I'd been to New York before, on visits with my parents. But Staten Island was a hit to the solar plexus. In DC, or at least in my DC, white folks were the minority. I never had to think about race.

But in one move, that all changed. My parents enrolled me in Catholic school, St. Joseph Hill Academy, located on a sprawling campus with rolling hills and an abundance of trees. My dad went to Catholic school as a kid, so sending me there was a no-brainer. On his side of the family, we come from a long line of devoutly Catholic Louisiana Creoles. My mom hailed from a long line of bourgie black Baptists—the kind of churches where no one shouts hallelujah or sings gospel—but she'd converted to Catholicism years before she met my dad. Enthusiastic Catholics liked to send their kids to Catholic school for the proper indoctrination. But more than anything, my parents, who were both products of a Jim Crow education, wanted me and my sisters to have the best education that money could buy.

Which is why, mere months after King's killing, I sat in my second-grade classroom at St. Joseph Hill, staring at my classmates, a sea of ruby-lipped kids with Italian and Irish last names.

My mother tells me that kids would pass out birthday-party invitations in class, skipping over me, and that she'd come up to school regularly, raising hell. Years later, a white classmate emailed me out of the blue to tell me that he remembered kids teasing me for being brown, and how I sat at my desk, stoic.

I don't remember any of that.

What I do remember is living life on mute. I retreated within, to the universe of my imagination, where the move was all a bad dream and that any minute I'd wake up and look and sound like everyone else. I'd learned to read when I was three, gobbling up Dr. Seuss and Grimm's fairy tales, comic books about Martin Luther King Jr., and anything else I could find. But suddenly, sitting in my new classroom, surrounded by all those ruby-lipped white kids, I couldn't remember the alphabet.

Everyone was white. I thought I'd glimpsed a black girl in the high school, but that might have been a mirage. The nuns were white, the crossing guards were white, and Father Rice, the resident priest who spoke with a thick Eastern European accent, was white too.

And, incredibly, they were all convinced I was Puerto Rican. No one asked me, of course. At recess, right in front of me, they would matter-of-factly talk about Puerto Ricans, and say, "You know, like Teresa." I have no idea what they were talking about in such a matter-of-fact way. All I heard was, "Puerto Rican, like Teresa." I didn't correct them. I didn't know how. I wasn't trying to perpetuate a fraud. I wasn't trying to pass. I just didn't have the words.

At home, my parents told me that we were black, that I should be proud. But they didn't tell me why I should be proud. Or maybe they did. I was quickly getting hip to this concept of race. There was a pecking order, and while being Puerto Rican wasn't really acceptable, it was a step up from being African American.

I absorbed this by osmosis. Every time someone had a case of mistaken identity with me or my family, from our babysitter to the people on the street who insisted on talking to my parents in Spanish, I felt like my blackness was this big, slightly shameful secret that I was lugging around. I never pretended to be anything else. Still, in my silence, I hid, right there in plain sight.

One person wasn't fooled, though.

Ernie was on to me. Puerto Rican—or was he Dominican?— Ernie, who was several shades darker than me, with a thatch of black curls brushed into submission. How did he know? Perhaps he'd been tipped off somehow—maybe his parents, noting that my German last name canceled out the *Latinidad* of my Spanish first name, pointed me out as not one of the clan.

The point was, he *knew*.

We sat there in class one day, the two lone brown kids. He hunkered behind me, whispering angry insults.

You're Negro, he hissed. You're Negro.

I didn't turn around.

I know, I hissed back.

So?

— — —

I wish I'd known then what I know now: That Puerto Rico and say, New Orleans, aren't all that different. That the slaveship express made stops all over Latin America too. That "Puerto Rican" and "black" were not mutually exclusive. That both Puerto Rico and the US had slavery and a legacy of rape. That I would travel to Puerto Rico and Cuba years later, rolling around in the richness of spoken Spanish, and marvel at the kinship I felt with strangers. Strangers who looked just like me.

That would come much later.

To seven-year-old me, Puerto Ricans were mysterious, those other brown people, who often spoke in a strange language and who clearly didn't like African Americans. Which meant that I didn't like them.

It took me years to get over that.

I'm a black woman with mixed-race roots, an amalgam of those who were enslaved and those who did the enslaving, with an American Indian ancestor or three thrown into the mix. I've spent a lifetime as a case of mistaken identity: I've been Puerto Rican/Dominican/Brazilian/Moroccan/Cuban/Pakistani/Indian/Arab/Yemeni/Ethiopian/Bangladeshi/Indonesian. Indonesian!

I've been a "spic."

A "fucking Hindu."

But never a "nigger."

At least, not to my face.

Not deliberately passing. But passing nonetheless.

Scroll back to the mid-'80s. I'm a young dancer, itching for a chance to travel abroad with a real dance company and get paid. New York. I'm at one of my first professional auditions. I'm on the sidelines, warming up at the barre. And I'm nervous. I'm also one of the few brown faces in the crowd, but I don't think much of it.

A woman with a clipboard comes up to me, looking concerned. "Do you speak English?" she asks. Enunciating carefully, she tells me that I was going to need a valid US passport to go on this tour. And apparently, I'd need to speak English too.

I don't get the job.

There is the Pakistani customs official at the Islamabad airport, who wants to know what I am. I am on my way back home from Afghanistan, covering life in Kabul in the midst of war for the *Washington Post*. I have been away for a month.

I am not in the mood.

I'm American, I tell him.

We know *that*, he says, gesturing impatiently at my passport. We want to know if you're *Pakistani* American.

I tell him I'm African American, but that only begets more questions, and I start to explain about slavery and forced amalgamation, and then I just stop.

It's a long story, I tell him.

Later that year, I am walking through the cobblestone streets of Antigua, Guatemala, on sabbatical from work, immersing myself for a few months in the language and culture of this beautiful and tragic country. Here, I've been temporarily gobsmacked by a crazy Chilean photographer with long braids, a goatee, and an abundance of tats. A devoted fan of rock and heavy metal, he's fond of telling me I'm just like Lenny, as in Lenny Kravitz, the only other light-skinned black American he's ever seen.

But today I am hanging out with a Nigerian doctor, who like me is here to improve his Spanish. He is tall and bald and very dark. I am small and brown with a headful of curls.

As we stroll through this colonial town, window-shopping, *Guatemaltecos* ride by, honking their horns and pointing at him.

They do this all the time, he says, resignedly. They don't mean anything by it. It's not hostile. They're just curious. I stand out.

I, on the other hand, do not stand out.

Here, I blend.

Blending sometimes has its advantages. Reporting in Pakistan and Afghanistan at a time when the white American journalist Danny Pearl was snatched and ultimately beheaded, blending in with the brown-skinned locals could be a matter of survival. Blending can also have its disadvantages. Like when I was harassed by the Havana police for riding in a cab with Americans and they were convinced that meant I had to be a *jinetera*, or high-class prostitute.

I'm American, I told them in deliberately bad Spanish. And then, and only then, did they leave me alone.

In Guatemala, no one pegs me for American. Unless, that is, they have reason to spot my passport. Some think I'm Cuban, others think I might be Colombian. But mostly, they think I'm Puerto Rican. When I insist I'm black, "Afro-Americana," they look at me quizzically, heads cocked. I don't fit their image of what an American looks like. American to them is blond hair and blue eyes. And African American is Kobe Bryant.

I could never ever pass for white. But I pass for other things, all the time. I am the child of two black parents who also pass for other things, all the time. My father, a bronze man with shiny jet-black curls, was once stranded in Egypt because they thought he was an Egyptian trying to flee the country with a fake American passport.

I am brown, yes, that olive-ish, Lena Horne Egyptian Tan frequently found in other ethnic groups/races. But it's more than just skin color that renders me the generic ethnic. As someone once said on a message board, when people are talking about light-skinned black folks versus dark-skinned black folks, skin color obviously plays a big part. But so too do facial features and hair texture. Like the rest of my family, my hair is curly, not kinky, my bumpy nose a racial Rorschach blot, inviting comparisons to everyone from Arabs to Germans to Blackfoot Indians.

Growing up and well into my twenties, I couldn't stand it when people asked me what I was. *What are you mixed with? Oh, come on, you couldn't be all black. Where are you from? No, where are you* really *from? Where are your parents from? You look like your mother is white and your father is black!*

I was trying to find my place in the racial firmament, amid constant reminders that I didn't fit in.

And yet, my DNA is as quintessentially American as you can get.

I'm black. And I'm a one-woman melting pot.

My family is full of stories like mine, complex stories of color and race.

— — —

I grew up worshipping my aunt, my mother's only sister. Marquelyn—her name is the feminization of my grandfather Marque's name—was only fifteen years older, which rendered her endlessly fascinating to me. She was grown up, but not really, a transitional figure between the mysterious world of grown-ups and my preschool world. I wanted to be her.

I remember her as tall and lean and pale and pretty, red-haired and green-eyed, at a time when Black was deemed Beautiful, a genetic throwback to our unnamed and unclaimed Scots-Irish ancestors. Growing up in Jim Crow Atlanta in the '50s and '60s, she was a rebel, taking advantage of genetics to cross the color line, ordering massive amounts of takeout at whites-only restaurants and bringing out the bounty for her darker-skinned buddies who waited outside, snickering at their little joke. At Spelman College, she acted in the theater department, painting scenery backstage, clad only in her slip, swigging a beer, while my scandalized grandmother, conducting a campus tour for some VIPs, pretended not to know her own daughter.

At three, I didn't know any of this, of course. But I sniffed out the rebel in her, for sure. Entranced and enchanted, I followed her everywhere, peppering her with questions, wiggling in delight whenever she deigned to call me "squirt."

After college, she married and moved to Phoenix, had a kid, divorced, and married again, both times to darker-skinned black men. She worked as an assistant principal and wrote plays, angry plays about racial discrimination and badass heroines who risked everything to take a stand. Then, even in lily-white Phoenix, her world was all black, from her hairstylists to her husbands to her friends to the art she made in her ceramics studio. Except for work, of course. She'd rail about her job, and all the white folks in this godforsaken town and all the racist bullshit she had to put up with.

I know they didn't want to see my black ass up in there, she'd huff.

And I'd just look at her, thinking, *How did they even know you were black?*

As the years passed, she distanced herself from my mother, my sisters, and me, save for the occasional stilted phone call. I still don't know why she stopped talking to us, to me. I went to see her twice before she died. Cancer, her fifth go-round. At the time, she could still talk, and so talk we did, about everything—except why she'd absented herself from our lives.

At her memorial service, the vast majority of people who came to pay their respects were white. One or two black folks, tops. Her best friend, a white woman I'd never met before, clutched my hand through the whole service, bawling. A slide-show showed me a side of Marquelyn I'd never seen: picture after picture of my usually sour-faced aunt hanging with white friends, laughing, looking happy. With her pale skin and reddish hair, she looked as white as they did.

She blended.

I have so many questions: What happened to my rebel aunt? Did she decide that being black took too much effort? What happened to all her black friends? Was this her ultimate rebellion? When she looked in the mirror, what did she see?

— — —

Fourth grade.

It's the early '70s, and it's hard to escape the heat and fury of energy of the time. The Black Panthers are nowhere near Staten Island, but they've made an impression. My parents, my mother, in particular, do whatever they can to take me beyond Staten Island. Just about every weekend, we are on the ferry, heading into Manhattan, to see black Broadway plays, black art, Alvin Ailey. Anything and everything to nurture a sense of racial pride.

The next year, *Soul Train* will save me. My cousins will visit me from Chicago, showing off their dance moves and their new curly 'fros. My dad will blast WBLS, the black radio station from Manhattan, and in so doing, turn me on to James Brown and Marvin Gaye and Sly and the Family Stone and the Supremes.

But that's next year. This year, I am nine and in the fourth grade. And I've already fallen in love with Michael Jackson and the Jackson 5, and on TV, *Sesame Street* and *Zoom* and *The Electric Company* show me a multiculti world of city kids, some of whom look a lot like me.

And there's a new kid in my class at St. Joseph Hill Academy.

I have spent the past two years there, without a best friend to call my own, feeling very much alone, hiding in my books.

Until Lucille. She's half-Irish, half-Italian, with long, curly brown hair and a snaggletoothed smile. She holds my hand, tight during recess, whispering secrets in my ear. You have to pry us apart.

She is the first classmate to invite me to a sleepover at her house. I am both excited and filled with dread. If she finds out my secret, will she rescind her invitation?

I have something to tell you, I say.

I'm Negro.

I'm *black*.

I know, she says, grabbing my hand and squeezing it. Hard.

Which Lie Did I Tell?

/ *Trey Ellis* /

I share the head of the table in the conference room in Columbia's Faculty House with a distinguished professor from USC. We are the featured guests for the latest Columbia University Seminar, a prestigious academic lecture series that has been running continuously since 1945. I am the invited "respondent/ discussant" for the presentation of Dartmouth professor Mark Williams's paper, "Passing for History: Humor and Early Television Historiography." All the serious, eminent professors and doctoral candidates lining each side of the table nod and take notes when Williams references visual and televisual "indexicality."

As soon as he finishes, we clap and immediately the array of eyes triangulate on my own. Outwardly, I spend a lot of time thanking everyone who can possibly be thanked. Inwardly, I obsess about my lowly and decades-old BA, my ignorance of the word *indexicality,* and how one of the assembled illuminati at any moment, surely in the middle of my talk, will burst to his feet and shout, like Congressman Joe Wilson at Obama's 2009 State of the Union address, "You lie!"

See, I'm not a real professor, but I play one in arts school.

I was invited to respond that night because I'd written a screenplay about the period discussed, and because thirty years earlier, soon after graduating college, I had written an essay called "The New Black Aesthetic," which has over the years allowed me a backdoor entrance into proper academic conferences such as this one. My actual job, as chair of screenwriting and associate professor of professional practice in the School of the Arts at Columbia University, is technically academic, but really arts academic, which is to say academic adjacent. Nevertheless, as I enter my ninth year of passing for a real prof, I find myself less and less inclined to correct those who mistakenly call me one.

You see, passing is like that. Real Harvard Business School professor and TED Talks rock star Amy Cuddy's advice to "fake it till you become it" is a corollary to long-term passing. Or, as veteran screenwriter William Goldman phrased it in the title of his second acidic Hollywood memoir, *Which Lie Did I Tell?*

I love that. *Which lie did I tell?* How do we remember how we crafted ourselves to an audience the last time we met them? Luckily, I've had years of practice. My adolescence as a black kid with a misshapen Afro in a working-class Italian and Irish suburb of New Haven, Connecticut, in the 1970s was a series of remembered lies, several of which continue to play out to this day. Passing through those years, I knew I was being contoured by the lies as they happened in real time. Of course, I had no idea to what end. In fact, the jury is still out. All I know is that thanks to my parents transplanting me often from one ethnic mix to another, I've become something of a code-switching connoisseur.

So at that Columbia seminar, despite my terror of being outed, the subject of the discussion was delicious to me. Thanks to Professor Williams's work, and the exhaustive research by legendary rock critic R. J. Smith, I learned about Korla Pandit, aka Cactus Pandi, aka Juan Rolando, aka John Roland Redd. Pandit was a kitsch fixture of Los Angeles television in the 1950s, a mesmerizing, bejeweled-turbaned Indian swami in a sharp Western suit. For fifteen minutes every evening, first locally and then nationally, he wordlessly seduced the camera, swaying and staring, almost as unblinking as the lens, while effortlessly noodling on his Hammond organ or a piano, sometimes at the same time, no sheet music, never looking down, as fluid orientalist melodies undulated from the keyboards as if Pandit were about to conjure endless ranks of grinning, dancing cobras.

Housewives swooned before his image: exotically light-brown, crowned in his tight bejeweled turban, never, ever speaking. The ultimate mystery man, from 1948 to 1953 he was becoming fabulously famous. Then, after a contract dispute with his syndicator, he was replaced by another keyboard player who went on to use the very same sets, only this guy was always smiling instead of cool and smoky, in white tie and tails, a lit candelabra reflected in the black gloss of the grand piano's lid. Pandit resented Liberace for the rest of his life.

Both of them were passing. Liberace as straight when he was gay, Korla as an Indian when he was a black St. Louisan born John Roland Redd.

John Redd had moved to Hollywood in the 1930s, and like all black musicians had to scrounge for gigs, since he was barred from the union. He then simply changed his name to Juan Rolando and started playing all over town. A few years later his identity crossed the South Atlantic to become Korla Pandit, a New Delhi–born musical prodigy, classically trained at the University of Chicago. The prodigy part was true: he was a brilliant and sought-after pianist for radio and high-profile Hollywood gigs. In the 1940s, he and his blond wife (they married in Tijuana where interracial marriages were not illegal) regularly partied with Errol Flynn and Bob Hope.

The LA TV show in the '50s was as high as his star ever rose. He moved his program to San Francisco for a few years, but eventually found himself dragging his organ to grocery store openings and piano lessons for kids. Then, thanks to the Tiki renaissance in the 1990s, he was rediscovered and again got regular gigs as a lounge act and even a cameo in Tim Burton's *Ed Wood*. When he died in 1998, even his children didn't know he was black.

What intrigues me most about John Redd is his asking us, to paraphrase Groucho Marx, not to believe our lying eyes. Conventional light-skinned black passing for white is easy enough. My high-yellow blue-eyed grandmother would routinely take grocery orders from all of her friends in the black section of Dayton, Ohio, break out her favorite platinum-blond beehive wig, and drive to the white side of town where prices were cheaper. The fact that a brown-skinned black man from St. Louis did it by adopting an exotic brown culture over his reviled black one, even circumventing the obstacle of a bad Indian accent by being mysteriously mute during the run of his show, is almost beyond genius.

As soon as I learned about Pandit, I wondered why more black folks hadn't tried it. The scam was as bold and as simple as that of Henry "Box" Brown, the slave who simply closed himself in a crate and shipped himself north to freedom. So in digging, I discovered a less famous but equally as clever black man passing as South Asian. Jesse Raymond Ruteé was a black preacher from Queens who, in the 1940s, would dress in elaborate robes and, yes, a turban from a costume store, before taking the train to visit his people down in Mobile, Alabama. Instead of being relocated with the rest of the black folks to the colored-only car as soon as the train crossed the Mason-Dixon Line, Pastor Ruteé was treated like a famous and exotic dignitary the entire trip, sitting and dining where he pleased. And unlike the bus section designated for blacks, the colored-only train car was in the front, bumpy and loud and covered in soot.

— — —

Every black person in America knows the intermittent lure of race denial. Bert Williams argued it well in his seminal essay "The Comic Side of Trouble" in *American Magazine* in 1918: "I have never been able to discover that there was anything disgraceful in being a colored man. But I have often found it inconvenient—in America." This incisiveness is especially heartbreaking coming from the vaudeville pioneer who made a living darkening his face with cork—a black man passing for blacker. His friend W. C. Fields famously said of Williams, "He was the funniest man I ever saw, and the saddest man I ever knew."

William Pickens, the brown-skinned field secretary of the NAACP in 1927, also understood the allure of race denial: "If passing for white will get a fellow better accommodations on the train, better seats in the theater, immunity from insults in public places, and may even save his life from a mob, only idiots would fail to seize the advantage of passing, at least occasionally, if not permanently."

Pickens's brother in arms, Walter White, NAACP executive secretary from 1931 to 1955, a black man who was 100 percent white-looking, could not have agreed less. In some respects, one could argue that White had spent his life passing for black. As he wrote in his autobiography, *A Man Called White*, "I am a Negro. My skin is white, my eyes are blue, my hair is blond. The traits of my race are nowhere visible upon me." White's honesty was admirable, and the questions he raised about blackness as culture versus physiognomy were asked again by Rachel Dolezal, the former and now disgraced white president of the Spokane, Washington, NAACP.

I've been obsessed with White since I started researching him, the chief villain in a film I've been writing about *Amos 'n' Andy*, the most popular radio show of all time, created and voiced by two white men, Freeman Gosden and Charles Correll, who for over thirty years passed for black on radio. Though they never hid their true identities, it constantly surprised them how many fans of all races were convinced they were actually black.

When the show finally came to TV in 1951, CBS flirted with the idea of using white actors in blackface, or Gosden and Correll voicing the parts while unknown black actors mouthed the words. Eventually, CBS was forced to cast black actors in the roles. Spencer Williams, the brilliant director of *Blood of Jesus*, would suddenly rocket to mainstream fame as TV's Andy Brown. He famously complained to Gosden, when the former tried to instruct him on how to sound more "colored," "You mean to tell me *a white man is trying to teach a Negro how to act like a white man acting like a Negro?!*"

Williams's dilemma is still familiar to every ethnic actor who's ever auditioned. White directors and casting directors routinely ask ethnic actors to accent their accents, if they have one, but more typically the actors are asked to adopt one from a trunk full of tired types, to pass as exotic when the actors are anything but. From Williams's lament to Robert Townsend's *Hollywood Shuffle* to Aziz Ansari's *Masters of None*, progress has been glacial to the point of imperceptibility.

In *Amos 'n' Andy,* Williams wasn't the only one whose authenticity was questioned. Early TV was of course in black and white and Alvin Childress, who played Amos to Williams's Andy, was a light-skinned black man. After a few episodes, CBS was afraid that in black and white, Childress could be confused for the latter, integrating the show, so they insisted on ridiculously dark face makeup for him. When you watch reruns on YouTube, look for the line on his neck where the brownface ends.

Passing again entered my work in my latest play. *Satchel Paige and the Kansas City Swing* is the story of Paige, one of baseball's

most legendary pitchers, and his bittersweet, complicated journey from the Negro Leagues to the Majors. When Paige was
young, white MLB baseball scouts were desperate to exploit his
talent and that of his peers. If the black ballplayers were light
enough, they would send them down to Cuba, have them learn a
little Spanish, apply a lot of skin-lightening cream, and pass them
off in the MLB as exotically Latino.

In fact, there was a team, the New York Cuban Giants, made
up entirely of African Americans who would speak rapid-fire,
accented gibberish to each other on the field to convince white
crowds they weren't garden-variety black Americans.

— — —

My obsession with all these historical subjects stems from my
own history of multivariable passing. Manet's *A Bar at the Folies-
Bergère* was an early revelation—perhaps the first time I looked
at a work of art and it looked back at me. It was my absolute
favorite painting in the Masterpiece board game my doctor- and
lawyer-in-training parents got for my sister and me to trick us
into absorbing high culture. No Chutes and Ladders, this; my
black tiger parents (*"A B is an F!"*) bought us a children's board
game about art history.

What resonated within me most about this overanalyzed
Manet wasn't the obvious trick of a painting of a mirror image:
the barmaid's sad gaze at the creepy rich guy (Manet himself?)
ogling her sadness while the dissipated frolic in the background.
What struck me instead was perspective. Subject and object. How
we are seen as we see. I couldn't help thinking of the barmaid
as me posing for my yearly elementary school photos. Inside,
I felt like all the other Italian, Irish, and Jewish kids. Inside, I
was unconsciously, seamlessly passing. But as soon as the photo
arrived in the mail, even *my* first thought was, *What's he doing*

there? That goofy-looking black kid. The photos always triggered
a song in my head: *One of these things is not like the other, one of
these things is not the same . . .*

The realization started shaping me. No matter how I was
feeling that day—nerdy, right-handed, gassy—the only descrip-
tor that would ever really matter would be my race. I was born
in 1962 at what was then Freedmen's Hospital in Washington,
DC, founded precisely a century earlier. Next to the campus
of Howard University, Freedmen's was the first hospital whose
explicit mission was to treat former slaves. My father was a Howard med student and we lived across the street. Freedmen's was
probably the most unadulteratedly black place to be born this
side of Harlem Hospital.

Things have been more mixed and murky ever since. My
family moved from black Dayton, Ohio, to blacker-than-black
Detroit in '65 and then to Ypsilanti, Michigan, in '68. In Ypsi,
in our neighborhood of still-being-built fake Tudor and semi-
attached townhomes, half of the families were young professionals or affiliated with the University of Michigan, while the other
half had dads working for GM's oceanic Willow Run assembly
plant. Maybe a third of us were black. The development and the
town was mixed enough that no one side could claim cultural
hegemony. For acceptance among my friends, no one had to pass
as anything except a great Hot Wheels track assembler.

When my father accepted a job as a psychiatrist to Yalies
at their student health services, my parents could have moved
us into New Haven proper, sort of a Detroit in miniature and
boasting one of the highest per capita homicide rates in the nation. Instead, they moved to one of its suburbs, Hamden, and
the white part of Hamden to boot. They told us it was because
they heard the schools were good for my sister and me, which
of course was part of it. But I suspect that as second-generation
college-educated black snobs, the most talented of the Talented

Tenth, they also thought they themselves had earned the right to escape the inner city.

Also, my mother was an aspiring playwright and a huge fan of *Raisin in the Sun*, and I believe the chance to live out that plot was too much for her to resist. Like Hansberry's Younger family in the late '50s, we Ellises in the 1970s were suburban pioneers, the only blacks actually living within the entire Spring Glen Elementary catchment area. Unlike the Youngers, there were no sidelong glances from the neighbors that I noticed, no bribes to get us to move. Or worse. Nobody burned a cross on our lawn when we arrived. That welcoming was reserved for black families trying to live over in Italian East Haven, where the news reported about a cross burning every year or so.

It was here in Hamden, as a true minority for the first time, that I began my lifetime of various passings. To my new Italian and Jewish friends, it wasn't initially my hue that drew their scorn. I was too new and we were so in the news for doing exactly what we were doing that my landing among them seemed ripped from the headlines. We were all living in our own ABC Afterschool Specials, and for the most part no one wanted to play the racist villain. But they were kids and had to attack difference, so instead it was my Midwestern flat *a*'s they savaged. My "pa-JAM-as," and "pop" instead of "soda," sent them cackling, so not only did I almost instantly erase those features from my speech, I was soon inserting their New England "Aw, wicked" into every possible utterance.

Though my sister and I were the only black kids living near school, a dozen or so other black kids were bused from the more depressed side of our depressed town. Since they left right after school, I didn't see much of them. It was about a month after I started that a black kid casually spat the word *Oreo* my way as he boarded his bus. A day later a white kid I didn't know hissed *nigger* while I was unlocking my bike.

I never brought these incidents to my parents. They would have marched on the school, especially my mom, dragged me kid to kid till I snitched. Instead I just swallowed it all and sulked. I withdrew into the persona of the silent sufferer, the tragic hero, the Melancholy Black Dane, Monet's self-pitying barmaid.

At Hopkins, the venerable private day school in New Haven, there were even fewer black kids than at Spring Glen: a handful of scholarship kids, and one or two middle-class strivers like myself. I was not good friends with any of them, convinced that my passing as a colorless, general-purpose nerd had been so successful that I had personally ushered the nation into a "postracial" world decades before the term even existed.

A few years later I transferred to Phillips Academy Andover, the boarding school of the Bushes, the Kennedys, the Goodyears, and the Rockefellers. The school gave every entering black kid the choice of a black roommate. Of course I declined. How pointless and backwards, I thought. When I arrived, I realized I was only one of two or three other black kids there who were not from the A Better Chance program, kids plucked from inner cities around the nation. But unlike at Spring Glen, we were all smart and thrilled to be living away from home. The AF-LAT-AM (Afro-Latino-American) house threw weekly dance parties with slow dancing toward the end of the night, so it was the nearness of black girls, specifically Joy Anderson, that started me sometimes venturing into black orbits. At Andover, surprisingly, individuality was so revered that groups were relatively fluid. Everyone, regardless of color or class, was convinced, by their mere acceptance into such a school, that their uniqueness was valued. Passing as anything other than yourself just seemed sad.

I arrived at boarding school determined to reinvent myself as the mysterious new kid. No one was fooled. I then begged my dad for Sperry Top-Siders. I was at the preeminent prep school, for God's sake. These shoes would telepathically instruct the Kennedys to invite me to Hyannis Port for Thanksgiving. A few weeks later, when he came up to visit, he surprised me with To-priders, plastic-soled knockoffs, the several-times-reduced price tag from Marshalls still on the box. And in the box they stayed.

Thanks to the black students I'd met at Andover, I entered Stanford radicalized. This time, not only did I request a black roommate, but the black dorm, Ujamaa! Actually it was only half-black by population, but it was the black cultural hub of campus. I was ready to reinvent myself again, and this time pass for an antiapartheid, red, black, and green cultural nationalist, a nonbourgy, non-boarding-school-educated black person. Unfortunately, however, my dad's high school graduation present was a pair of real Top-Siders, and I made the mistake of wearing them to Ujamaa my first day in college.

A black girl, beautiful, of course, actually stopped me in the hall and gaped.

"What *are* those on your feet?"

Day One and I was instantly branded the black preppy Republican/narc living in a dorm where the RA unironically wore a dashiki. It was an endless and alienating freshman year, and besides my roommate, my best friends in the dorm were some of the white kids who were thrown into Ujamaa by chance, and as much outsiders as myself.

The next year I left for the school's campus in Italy, a Renaissance villa with manicured gardens on a hill high above Florence. Michelangelo used to hang out there. As usual, I was the only black kid, though there were about seventy of us. Most of the kids barely spoke the language and left the villa mainly to go to the train station and travel the continent. I moved out after a semester with a friend to live in the city, and not only did I learn to speak, I affected a Florentine accent that never ceased to make them smile. Like moving from Michigan to Connecticut, being in Italy triggered my internal chameleon, my autonomic passing reflex.

And I loved it. I moved back to Florence after graduation to finish *Platitudes,* my first novel, and I got a perverse kick whenever I was mistaken for something more exotic than an American Midwesterner. I rented a very small room in Scandicci, a working-class suburb, and I remember coming out of the *alimentari,* the Italian version of a bodega, joking with the owner, when an extremely old and twiggy Italian woman suddenly clutched me and said, "Uno dei nostri Somali!"

One of our Somalians. This was so fucked up on so many levels. The Italians had colonized Somalia and neighboring Ethiopia very, very badly. Her casual use of the possessive pronoun epitomized the evils of colonialization, something I knew a lot about, since several of my friends in Italy were actual Somali students.

Nevertheless, I was proud that I had been able to trick her. And to be fair, years later, both in Ethiopia and in LA's Little Ethiopia, Ethiopians often come up to me speaking Amharic.

Back in Italy, just out of college, I was only beginning to understand my ability to choose how I was viewed by others. I imagine Korla Pandit did it much better. Since then, I have been struggling to perfect the masks I wear, with the goal of being able, like the members of the Impossible Mission Force, to reach under my chin and peel them off at will.

Thirty years later, I am just now coming not to care how I am judged, not because of some inner strength, but the realization of the futility of caring about it. We're all judged by such complex matrices that it is impossible to anticipate them all. I'm only now coming to a place Joan Armatrading arrived at in 1979 with her lyric from the song "How Cruel": *I heard somebody say her black was way too black . . . and someone answer she's not black enough for me.*

If you can't win, stop playing.

— — —

These issues and variants of passing swirled, unformed, in my head for years before they began to coalesce. Finally, a working theory on identity and identity politics, and what got me invited to speak at the Columbia University Seminar, began in earnest in a black studies survey course my senior year in college. It was 1983 and we had been reading Addison Gayle's 1972 anthology, *The Black Aesthetic*. Although many of the essays spoke to me, so many others seemed essentialist, defining blackness as some clunky combination of African and not-white. It was as a mid-term paper in that class that I shaped my "New Black Aesthetic" essay, revised and published in *Callaloo* six years later and leading me to the term *cultural mulatto*. In that essay I wrote, "Just as a genetic mulatto is a black person of mixed parents who can often get along fine with his white grandparents, a cultural mulatto, educated by a multi-racial mix of cultures, can also navigate easily in the white world." Our freedom from essentialist labeling had freed us as artists to steal, meld, satirize, and reconstitute from the best of every culture on the globe.

Of course, much of my youthful bravado was an act. I was passing as if I didn't give a shit. In fact, I still remember the tightening in my chest when I self-described as mulatto. I knew the word came from the Portuguese for "little mule"—half horse, half ass—knew very well how we elevate mixed kids, especially biracial women, with what part-whiteness does to hair and noses. I knew that we garden-variety black folks weren't supposed to revere or at least envy their ambiguity.

The beginning of the essay came easily. I knew more about the workings and influence of American and European culture than did a large majority of white Americans, while much of what I knew about the lives of inner-city black folks was what I saw on *Good Times*. Why couldn't I claim and steal influences at will?

Like most every African American, I certainly had some white in me. To varying degrees, we are almost all that mix of African, white, and Cherokee that hundreds of years of cohabitation engenders. Who among us doesn't have that great-grandmother with a long braid down her back? A meriny-skinned uncle who challenged you to count his freckles? Besides my blue-eyed grandmother on my father's side, weren't my Virginia- and Philadelphia-based mother's family proud descendants of the Delaware Indians? When my son was in the third grade at New York City's PS 87, I was so thrilled when he informed me that the Delaware were also known as the Lenape, also known as the tribe that sold Manhattan to the Dutch for sixty guilders (not a single trinket or bead).

I knew there was a special reason I loved my Manhattan! From the moment I had moved here in the tenth grade I instantly felt so at home. The city was literally mine! My surgeon sister was convinced that if we could prove our Native Americanness we wouldn't have to pay taxes. So she spat in a tube and sent it off to Ancestry.com.

"Trey. Um. There must be a mistake. I need you to get tested."

She was 49 percent white.

"And how about Indian?"

"Please. I'll pay for it."

So I spat into my own tube and four weeks later discovered that I was made up of several different pieces, the largest of which was, unsurprisingly, West African: Ghanaian/Ivory Coast/ Nigerian/Cameroonian/Congolese and Senegalese, about 40 percent. However, the single-largest group by far, twice as much as Ivory Coast/Ghana, was Irish, at 31 percent. And

Native American? Zero. *Zero!* It said I was 2 percent Scandinavian! Two percent Finnish/Northwest Russian! How could I have no Native blood at all?

And while my freckle-faced, light-skinned sister was 49 percent white, my Irish, Scandinavian/Finnish/Western European/ Iberian Peninsula/Italy/Greece/Great Britain and Eastern European DNA totals added up to 51 percent of who I am. A majority holding. *WTF?* I'm fifty-three years old, have been writing and thinking about race and race identity for over thirty years, and only now do I find out I have been passing all my life. Half horse, half ass.

Negroland

/ *Margo Jefferson* /

When Uncle Lucious stopped being white, my parents invited him to dinner. He had worked for decades as a traveling salesman, making periodic contact with his sisters and with cousins who looked white enough to meet him in segregated places when he came to town. Then he retired, and his retirement community was Negroland.

Denise and I were told the basic story, and we greeted him politely. I watched him covertly all evening. He had the long Jefferson face. But I could find no—*no*—physical sign that he was a Negro. His nose was blade-straight, his lips sliver-thin, his skin nearly as white as his hair. I told myself, *We have friends who look as white as Uncle Lucious.* But I had always known them as Negroes. The word had kept its visual fluidity, even as it acquired social obligations and political constraints. Now I was in free fall. Who and what are "we Negroes," when so many of us could be white people? I sat there and reasoned it out: if I am related to Uncle Lucious and I am visibly Negro and Uncle Lucious is invisibly Negro and visibly white . . . Suddenly the fact of racial slippage overwhelmed me. I was excited for days after. I knew something none of my white school friends knew. It wasn't just that some of us were as good as them, even when they didn't know it. Some of us *were* them.

Our cousin Lillian Granberry Thompson looked as if her portrait could hang in the Museum of the Confederacy. ("Lillian," she said her father always told her, "the best blood of Mississippi runs in your veins.") She was a few years older than my father and chose to live as a fair-skinned Negro, passing for convenience when she wanted to patronize white-only shops and restaurants; reaping the little rewards (deference here, flattery there) often granted her by brown-skinned Negroes. She was a trusted conduit between the passers and the nonpassers in Daddy's family.

So many in my parents' world had relatives who'd spent their adult lives as white people of some kind. Avocational passing was lighthearted. Shopping at whites-only stores, getting deferential service at whites-only restaurants. You came home snickering: *What fools these Nordics be!* Passing-for-life stories were melodrama prompts. P. lived as a Negro woman severed from her twin brother, who lived as a white man; N. was the only child in a family of eight to remain a Negro; H.'s brother had spent decades as a white man in a small English town; when his passworthy niece and I went to Europe the summer before we were college seniors, she visited him without me. Our mothers had discussed it beforehand.

That was when Daddy told me about our cousin J.E., who'd passed as a successful white business and family man somewhere in the Midwest. I use initials to shield his public identity. His mother, my great-aunt Bessie, lived in Chicago. He would sometimes make contact with Cousin Lil when he came to town (he had risen to the top or near top of an insurance company); then she'd call other Negro relatives to set up visits. In my father's telling, the conversation was highly elliptical: "A childhood friend's in town and would like to see you—can we come by your office tonight when you've finished work?"

He even lowered his voice as he told the story. As I reconstruct it: Night has fallen. The patients have gone home, the nurse and receptionist have gone home. There's a knock on the door. Cousin Lil enters first; she and my father kiss each other's cheeks; she is followed by J.E. Do they hug or shake hands? Shake hands, I imagine, then (maybe a second's hesitation?) trade upper-arm pats. "How you doing?" "Fine, fine. Good to see you." If it's winter, talk of Chicago's cold will get them past the first awkwardness; if it's spring or summer, the heat leads to reminiscing about their Southern childhood.

"What did you talk about?" I asked. "We talked about the old days," my father said, gazing past me. The old days, when they were all Mississippians with parents listed as "mulattoes" on the local census forms.

Why did J.E. choose to visit Daddy? Had they been especially close or was this just one visit? I didn't ask. It was as if the visit, like J.E.'s life, has to be sealed off, as if further conversation would record what must stay hidden. Daddy told me that J.E.'s white sons had gotten wind of his ancestry when he died. Was that because his wife had known or suspected? Has there been a deathbed confession? Did the boys find incriminating documents when they went through his papers? How did they find a trail that led back to Rust, the Negro college he'd attended in Mississippi before transferring to the University of M—— up north? They were thwarted at Rust, told of a fire that had destroyed a number of school records, including their father's. Was this true, or were school administrators old hands at putting white relatives off the scent of ex-Negroes? The sons persisted, somehow made their way to Chicago, where they presented themselves at their grandmother's, only to be rebuffed. How did they introduce themselves? Did they speak timidly, courteously, or gruffly and accusingly? Did they show her a photograph of the son and father who had thrown their patrimony into such doubt? I was told nothing except that she gave the answer her son would have wished. "I've never heard of that man," she said, and closed the door.

Melodrama demands a climactic tableau.

Tableau of Resolve—the Mother, defiant, preternaturally still, her voice a low telltale throb—and of Consternation: let's have one son rearing back, shocked and confounded; the other turning away, hand to chest, every muscle conveying "Thank God! I've been reprieved."

Melodrama recedes as my cousins resume their old lives or assume new ones. What had J.E. and his wife taught them about the Negro race? What did they know of Negroes before Negroness was thrust upon them? This will affect their decision. Together or apart, they can go on being white men who no longer have the privilege of taking themselves for granted. Or they can take on the touchy, hyperconscious identity of light, bright, damn-near-white Negroes. Either way, no surface will ever be superficial again.

Uncle Lucious didn't come to our house again. I have a picture of him on my father's cabin cruiser, the *Bali Ha'i*. He sits next to his sister. He looks content; she looks ebullient. My father told me that once he settled in he began to telephone his Negro relations and accuse them of neglecting him. Psychologically transparent. But he'd been a prickly white man too, said my father, regularly disturbing his own peace by getting into fights when he heard people mock or demean Negroes, as he inevitably did at the white bars and restaurants he invariably went to. "They don't talk about anything but us. What we do, how we look, how much they hate us," he told my father. But they must have talked about something else *sometime*. And the ordinary talk of ordinary white men must have been a comfort to Uncle Lucious in those early days. He could handle the nasty turns at first. Till he couldn't. Then he'd fuss and fight and make himself a target of anger. Of suspicion. So when the time came to retire, he retired, retreated, and resettled among Negroes. But he wasn't really a Negro anymore. He was a former white man. And my parents looked down on him a little. Not because he'd passed, but because he'd risen no higher than traveling salesman. If you were going to take the trouble to be white, you were supposed to do better than you could have done as a Negro.

Slipping into Darkness

/ Lisa Page /

"**D**o you mind if I tell people your mother was married to a black man?"

Kelly is a white woman, about my age, who was my mother's good friend. My sister and I are with her in my mother's apartment in Chula Vista, Mexico. We're here to plan a memorial service and settle her affairs. She's lived in Mexico for twenty years. Kelly was one of her closest friends. She'd had no idea my sister and I are biracial.

"Tell who you want," I say, but feel a familiar stab of shame. This isn't the answer my mother would want me to give.

I sit at a glass kitchen table next to medications, packets of Sweet'N Low, and my mother's oxygen mask. She has been dead a week. The floor is clean and so is the table, indicating the caregiver cleaned up, before we arrived. Everything else is covered with a tinge of dust and disuse. A blue-rimmed vase holds yellow eucalyptus. Insects collect in a basket against the wall.

"How long were your parents married?" Kelly asks.

"About eight years."

We shift in our chairs. Embroidered pillows from India are propped on the couch along with a knit throw from Guatemala. The piano sits, closed, in the next room.

"She told me she was divorced and had three children. She never said anything about anything else."

My sister and I exchange looks. This is not new information. Her ashes arrive in an elegant box made of wood.

— — —

People steal looks at us as the service begins. We're at the American Foreign Legion on the shoreline of a large natural lake. I realize we look more like the local population than like our mother. Her friends are self-professed "gringos," white retirees who sit in fold-up chairs on the patio facing the street. They are from the States, Canada, and the UK, and form a large expatriate community here. A Mexican man with his disabled son is begging outside a locked gate. One of the guests walks over and insists they leave.

My sister stands and talks about how happy our mother was to spend her last years in a country she loved. Her friends also stand and remember her love for the Maya. They talk about time spent with her, in Mexican art galleries and restaurants. My brother and I do not stand to talk at all.

How can I possibly say what I feel? Her friends are kind but unware that, to the very end, she was ashamed of us. Our showing up in this Mexican town outs her one final time. But there's no pleasure in it. No satisfaction.

We serve sandwiches and ice water. We thank everyone for coming. Afterwards, we sip drinks at the bar.

My mother passed as a white woman without a black ex-husband. As a mother without biracial children. In Mexico, she became someone new.

— — —

My parents met in Chicago, in the 1950s. She was a social worker on the West Side of the city. My father, Grady, was a pharmacist at the neighborhood drugstore. He made her something at the soda fountain—phosphate and syrup, foaming over ice—every time she came in. He loved to talk over a cold drink about his other job, playing saxophone in his own jazz band. He was barrel-chested, with high cheekbones, and stood just shy of six feet tall. He had the kind of laugh that was contagious. She was as tall as he was, with blond hair and green eyes. Freckles marked her face and arms. She loved music and played classical piano. She had put herself through college, playing piano for a ballet school. One rainy night, he gave her a ride home.

When they started courting, interracial marriage was illegal in twenty states. But segregation never got in my father's way when it came to women. He lived in a segregated world—Alabama first, then Chicago—yet interracial relationships were nothing new for him. His own mother was biracial—what he called "mixed"— and his paternal grandparents were West Indian and Seminole. His maternal grandmother passed for white in Mississippi and got a college education. White women were not unusual in his crowd of musician friends that included Charlie Parker, Sonny Stitt, and Eddie Lockjaw Davis.

The opposite was true for my mother. She grew up in a western Michigan factory town where the railroad tracks divided the whites from the blacks. Her father was uneducated and Pennsylvania Dutch. Her German mother was a fan of Adolf Hitler in the 1930s. My mother—born Margaret and known as Marge—lived in a white world with white privilege, never questioning her access to parts of the country my father could never step foot in.

In Chicago she found a sophisticated city where rules were sometimes broken along the color line but other boundaries remained in place. Marshall Field's, downtown, didn't hire colored people. My father couldn't buy a business on the North Side because of redlining that divided the city, legally, along racial lines. When he bought his own drugstore, it was in Bronzeville, Chicago's version of Harlem, on the South Side. His out-of-town jazz musician friends—Miles Davis, John Coltrane, Cannonball Adderley—could play the North Side clubs but had to sleep on the South Side in black hotels.

My mother and father hung out at the Beehive, the Rhum-Boogie Café, and the Club DeLisa. He was on the bandstand, while she sat at a table smoking cigarettes, her blond hair illuminated by the spotlight.

My mother's parents met my father for the first time at the wedding ceremony. Until the moment Marge and Grady said their vows, her parents wouldn't acknowledge their interracial relationship.

I was born a year later. My mother was given a room in the maternity section of what is now the University of Chicago Medical Center. When my father showed up, mother and child were suddenly transported to the colored maternity ward of the hospital. She was on the flip side of the segregated society she had always lived in but never understood. My mother was no longer just a tourist on the black side of town.

She was devastated. She felt discounted, erased. Seven years later, she filed for divorce. My father resisted. He argued that she was being irrational. By then they had three children together. But their problems went way beyond their racial differences. She had a white boyfriend and plans for a new future. She stopped going to hear jazz in nightclubs. She never had black friends again.

— — —

It was clear I was mixed with something. White people wanted me to explain what was going on. Black people did too.

We stood out when we visited my mother's family. The three of us were dark-haired and olive-skinned, while our cousins in

Michigan were mostly fair and blue-eyed. Occasionally we were mistaken for white, which pleased my mother. My father's bloodline was an unfortunate detail she had put behind her. Her family wouldn't live in denial, however. They vacillated between deciding which was my mother's bigger sin: race mixing or divorce. Family reunions meant two sets of group photographs: one set that included us and the other without. My uncle told his neighbors our mother was a widow who'd lost her East Asian husband in the war.

My grandfather decided to clarify things. His false teeth meant he had no lips, so when he spoke, his mouth was two wet lines that opened and closed. His blue eyes shone behind his glasses.

"You'll never be as dumb as colored people," he said with a smile, sitting my sister and me on his lap, "because you're half-white. But you'll never be as smart as white people because you're half-colored."

My childhood self took this to mean that I was split, fueled by two genetic pipelines. My black side was inferior. My white side was superior. This idea was reinforced by my mother, who won custody of us in the divorce. We were so lucky, she insisted, to be raised by her instead of our father. Yet, the older I got, the more ridiculous this seemed. Even as I certainly got that, where my grandfather was concerned, we were substandard. Defective. Even subhuman.

The term "African American" didn't exist back then. This was before black was beautiful. "Negro" was the polite version of a much more common word. Our growing up was laced with shame. These memories mean a closing of the throat, the aura before the migraine, the stab of light in the corner of your eye. I was almost acceptable. Light enough. But flawed.

I was mistaken for everything I wasn't: Puerto Rican, Italian, Greek, Dominican, Mexican, Jewish. My ethnicity was either a question or an assumption. People didn't connect me with my mother. I had to tell people we were related.

I wasn't blond. I wasn't white. I was mixed. I learned early that ambiguity along racial lines made people uncomfortable. So I worked to make people comfortable by passing for whatever they wanted me to be. The question I heard the most often was: Are you black or white? When I answered I was both, I learned this was unacceptable. Many times, people told me to figure out who I was.

But first, I passed. I did it consciously. That was my job: to figure out just exactly who you wanted me to be. And once I figured it out, I supplied it, in spades. Was I light-skinned and bourgeois? Exotic and sassy? Black? White? Intelligent? Stupid? I was only too happy to oblige. Passing was my modus operandi. My ticket in to the rest of the world.

— — —

I'd been to Chula Vista once before. It was the last time I saw my mother alive. Throughout my youth, she had a series of break-downs. This one landed her in the hospital.

We were told the gardener heard her crying for help. He found her on the floor of the kitchen, unable to walk, severely malnourished and dehydrated. She was rushed to the hospital where, in a delusional state, she tried to pull the IV out of her arm.

My sister and I flew to Guadalajara and drove to Ajijic. The Nahuatl Indians named the area Ajijic, before the Spanish came. It means "the place where the water springs forth." Our mother always loved living near water. Lake Michigan was replaced by this new body, in Mexico. We took in a landscape framed by the Sierra Madre on one side and Lake Chapala, the largest fresh-water lake in Mexico, on the other. Purple petals littered the sidewalks from the jacaranda branches overhead. Tree trunks along the *carretera* were painted white to ward off animals and insects. Ants, we were told, could strip a tree overnight. We maneuvered around donkeys and the road was full of *topes*—speed bumps—to slow down the trucks, jeeps, and motorcycles. We drove through Ajijic's surrounding areas: Las Forrestas, San Antonio, and Chula Vista.

My mother was at a small hospital called Clinica Mascaras on the *carretera*. She looked terribly small under the sheets. The skin on her arms hung like rope off her bones. It wasn't clear to the doctors what happened to her. Was it a stroke? A heart attack? A psychotic break?

"I had a really good friend who died," she answered. "Her death really upset me."

She was propped up against a pillow. Her hair was matted around her head.

"She was the only one I told."

"Told what?" I asked.

"About you."

"What about me?"

"About you kids. Your father. I don't think it's anybody's business."

Her words cut me. But I was there to assist, not to settle old scores. By then, we had been estranged for years. My sister, Leslie, had a better relationship with her. And so I mirrored Leslie as she sat, smiling, on the other side of the hospital bed.

After that, we drove to her *casita*, where we would stay until we found assisted living for her. It was a beautiful but roach-infested two-bedroom cottage in a small housing development. Inside the *casita* was a wood-burning fireplace, two walk-in showers, and terra-cotta floors. Palm and pine trees grew outside, as well as croton Norma, white oleander, bougainvillea, and hibiscus. My mother deeply loved tropical gardens. I imagined her on the stone patio, next to the saltwater pool. A *palapa* with a thatched roof hung over the lawn chairs. There was a hammock and a glider.

We went in search of dinner. Mexicans sold their wares near Super Lake grocery, down the cobblestone alley behind the *casita*. Some sold fresh peaches in baskets and silver jewelry on the street. I imagined my mother making this same walk, every day. Now her doctor said she couldn't walk and should never live alone again. He recommended round-the-clock care and that we find assisted living for her.

We found a restaurant and ate a supper of enchiladas as we talked about our plan of action.

— — —

My mother became someone new in 1992. She was able to do this when she retired. She sold the Chicago townhouse, invested the money, and lived off the interest for the rest of her life. She moved from the South Side of Chicago, where our family was known, to Mexico, where she had no history.

In Mexico, Marge became Marni. Marni is the name of a high-end clothing line originally founded by Consuelo Castiglioni in 1994. Some will also remember the late Marni Nixon, who worked in Hollywood as a ghost singer, supplying her voice, in secret, to Audrey Hepburn, Marilyn Monroe, and Natalie Wood, among others. It's also the name of the title character in the Alfred Hitchcock film *Marnie.*

Hitchcock adapted it from a novel by Winston Graham about a woman who embezzles for a living until she is caught by one of her employers. He blackmails her into marrying him. The film stars Tippi Hedren and Sean Connery. The opening scenes show a dark-haired Hedren on a train platform with a suitcase, wearing dark glasses. The camera pans on an executive complaining about the money she stole from his company. Then the camera cuts back to a hotel room where Marnie is washing out her black hair dye in the sink. Suddenly she's a blond. She removes the back of her compact and pulls out Social Security cards with different aliases. She chooses one and inserts it into a new wallet. Marnie strips away her past—she literally washes the "black" out of her hair—and reinvents herself.

My mother introduced me to all of Hitchcock's films. We watched them, together, on television. We both loved Marnie's reinvention as well as her facility in the corporate world. Marnie did what she wanted. When trouble loomed, she put on a disguise—one she could remove if she chose to.

My mother washed out the darkness—her children, her marriage—and became Marni in Mexico. Blond and squeaky clean.

She severed herself from her past, but passing is a complex business. You sacrifice your identity for mobility but you also sacrifice yourself. You can't be all the things you really are. You have to conform. And that conformity is a cultural adjustment. In Hitchcock's film, Marnie is caught in her game of deception. She has to face herself.

My mother passed by omission. Marni "didn't think it was anyone's business" who her ex-husband was or what color her children happened to be. Our existence became her secret. She worked strenuously to not reveal the past.

My sister and brother remained closer to her than I did following her move to Mexico. By then I was married to an African American man. I couldn't stomach her tacit disgust over who I was. She didn't approve of my marriage or of my giving birth to a boy named after my father. I was slipping into darkness, as far as she was concerned. Embracing a world of obscurity and deprivation.

"You'll always live a second-class life," she admonished. "You could do so much better."

Once she was settled in Mexico, my siblings went to see her. Their first visit was a rough awakening. A white neighbor dropped by while they were in the living room. My mother made my siblings hide in the back while she opened the door. She wouldn't invite the neighbor in. The reason was clear.

After that she preferred to meet all of us in neutral places, usually Puerto Vallarta or the Riviera Maya. I went once. I brought my family with me. We both made an effort to be civil. Which felt like progress.

When my husband acquired some fame by appearing on public affairs television shows, she changed her mind about him. She even told her gringo friends I was married to him. She didn't reveal that I was a person of color too. It was OK if her friends believed I was white, because in her mind I *was* white. I was her daughter. No one needed to know the details.

She always expected me to go along with the program and pass for white. That was her plan, even as I'm sure she never said the words out loud. Given the option to live in the white world— the better world, in her mind—surely I knew which way was up. It never occurred to her that I might want something else.

My brother and sister were more compliant. Some would say they passed for white, but I don't think they ever did, intentionally. They were inside a culture they knew from the start.

I had something they didn't. Because I was the firstborn, I had more time, living with my father. For me, he was the bright side of our family tree.

— — —

Forgiveness. I heard the word many times but I wasn't interested. I told people I was finished with my mother. I spent holidays with my father and my stepmother in Chicago. Raised my son in Washington, DC. He knew he had a white grandmother and met her a handful of times.

Then I learned she was dying. She had colon cancer, but her primary physician didn't make the diagnosis until it was too late. She wanted to talk to me.

Our conversations were pragmatic at first. What did her doctor say? What was the prognosis? She didn't like it when I told her to get a second opinion or that I wanted her to go to a hospital in Guadalajara. What did I know?

Her physical condition declined very quickly. She did rounds of ineffective chemo and even resorted to scorpion venom.

She started asking me to come to Mexico. She was frightened of death, which she knew was close. In our last conversation, the phone kept giving off feedback. Sucking sounds. Rattling noises. Weird reverberations. It was a bad connection. The static felt like the underworld was inserting itself into our conversation.

"Do you forgive me, Lisa?" she asked.

— — —

We stay at La Nueva Posada, in Ajijic, following the service. It's a boutique hotel my mother loved, thanks to its lush, tropical garden and view of the lake. It has a restaurant with a patio overlooking the water. The restaurant is called La Rusa after a Russian ballerina who also retired in Ajijic. I wonder if she also lived with secrets.

A huge rubber tree is in the center of the patio, full of lights hanging over the tables. A caged bird sings along the walkway. The inside of the hotel is full of cut glass, *equipales*, and Spanish Colonial archways. Cannons fire in the morning to celebrate Our Lady of Guadalupe. We watch an egret walk along the rocky shoreline. And I think of Marge who became Marni in Mexico, who strolled through galleries, drank margaritas, and laughed with the gringos. A woman who loved the Maya and hid the African blood that flowed in her children's veins for twenty years.

My mother found a new life here. It came with a price, but then, secrets often do. She thought the price was worth it. Whatever the circumstances, I am glad she found a place that gave her pleasure at the end of her life.

My husband is with me. We have drinks on the patio and stroll through the *tiendas* in the late afternoon. The light in the streets is blinding.

Among the
Heterosexuals

/ *M. G. Lord* /

I admire Nora Ephron. For over a decade I have assigned her brilliant essay on not being Dorothy Parker in every creative-nonfiction class I have taught. But when the word "passing" comes to mind—a charged word that suggests deceit around racial identity or sexual orientation—I think of her.

Not that Ephron passed for anything. To me she was as pure and authentic as a person could be. But in 1985, when I was a young writer at *Newsday,* I was not so pure and authentic. Nor had I yet published any critically acclaimed books. Ephron had no reason to befriend me, as she would ten years later, when my book, *Forever Barbie: The Unauthorized Biography of a Real Doll,* came out. Ephron put a Barbie doll in one of her movies. We stayed in touch until her death.

In 1985 I was an unknown, struggling to do a story about women and comedy pegged to the opening of Lily Tomlin's one-woman show on Broadway. No one considered important would talk to me. I was, however, living with an influential man,

who asked his friend, the novelist Joseph Heller, to nudge Ephron to speak with me by phone, which she did.

At first we spoke in general terms about comedy. "If you slip
on a banana peel," she told me, "other people can make fun of
you. But if you tell the story about slipping, you own the story.
It's your joke now."

We moved on to Tomlin, whom Ephron esteemed, talking
about her curious commitment to keeping her lesbianism a secret. I had heard that Tomlin had been up for a part in *Silkwood*,
the 1983 movie that Ephron wrote with Alice Arlen and that
Mike Nichols had directed. Ephron confirmed that Tomlin was
considered for the part of Dolly Pelliker, a lesbian who shared a
house with nuclear whistleblower Karen Silkwood, the title character, played by Meryl Streep, and her boyfriend, Drew Stephens,
portrayed by Kurt Russell. Then Ephron starkly explained the director's choice: "We didn't want one who *was* one to play one."

My jaw dropped. Actually, it didn't drop—and such dropping would not have mattered, as we were on the phone. I was
as composed as a rock. But I felt something inside me sink.

In this moment I began to understand the tawdry word: *passing*. I understood that it allowed people to assume I was a member of a privileged group—in this case white arty heterosexuals
who summer in the Hamptons. If Ephron had had the vaguest
clue that I might have been a lesbian—that I was recovering from
the recent random murder of a woman I had deeply loved—she
would never, ever have used such cavalier language. She would
have been gracious and sensitive, because she *was* gracious and
sensitive. But there I was—a pretty white twentysomething apparently about to marry a successful man with an antiquarian
business in the city and many clients in eastern Long Island. She
made an obvious assumption. I had "passed." I had a window
into a world I wasn't sure I wanted to see.

— — —

Blessedly, much has changed since 1985. Few in educated circles engage in casual homophobia, though I am still often shocked by the crude, anonymous comments on the Internet. Although there are exceptions, in civilized company, both straight and gay people struggle to avoid transphobia. The '70s and '80s, however, were a brutal, discriminatory time. Few people thought twice about using raw language to express bigoted ideas. My story is set in the '80s, and it may be as much about that decade as it is about me. I didn't slip on a banana peel. My story isn't hilarious. But I took Ephron's advice: I own this story. I don't want it told uncharitably by an outsider.

— — —

Passing involves deliberateness, which makes my authentic yet conflicted foray into heterosexuality all the more confusing, and maybe even sad. Passing is studied and intentional. I know this because I once tried to pass as something that I wasn't. As a Yale freshman from an undistinguished West Coast public high school, I tried to be a chameleon. I didn't throw away the embroidered peasant blouses and denim bellbottoms that I had worn at home. I kept them to pass with hippie-identified Yalies. But being a flawed person, a person who had read *This Side of Paradise* way more often than a peasant child should, I was intrigued by the upper tiers of Ivy League society—the glittering private school kids, who stood out in part because of the rigid coding of their clothes. They wore things I had never even seen in the surfer-hippie slum where I grew up: Top-Siders, duck boots, pastel polo shirts with small embroidered alligators, and Fair Isle sweaters that looked, when new, as if a small animal had been trapped inside and stretched random sections of wool in a fierce effort to get out.

In October of freshman year, a well-meaning but blunt-spoken acquaintance from Farmington (or another women's boarding school—I could not keep track of them back then) buttonholed me outside my residence hall. "Don't take this the wrong way," she said. "I like you. You have a lot going for you. But you're not in California anymore. You need to stop dressing like a migrant farmworker." Yes, I know: no socially conscious undergraduate in 2016 would use "migrant farmworker" as a casual slur. But this was 1973. I let her take me shopping.

We went to J. Press, a fusty emporium unchanged since the 1930s. But I might be misremembering. Coeducation was so new back then that few old-line stores stocked women's clothes. Eventually, I lugged home a boxy Fair Isle sweater, several oxford-cloth shirts, and khakis. Then we hit the mall for a black cocktail dress and unassuming pumps, to replace the unsafe platform heels that my fashion arbiter had pronounced "preposterous." A man who regularly wore multiple Lacoste shirts at the same time had invited me to a dance at the Fence Club, a museum of prep life in the 1950s, a bastion against the left-wing politics of Yale during Watergate. As you might imagine, I did not seamlessly fit in. But I at least looked the part. And through a miracle of fate—I had had to take ballroom dancing lessons in junior high—I even managed to pass on the dance floor. But passing, as Professor Henry Higgins knows well, is as much about attitude as appearance. I could never cultivate the insouciance that comes from having a million-dollar trust fund. I felt as if I had my financial aid forms pinned to my clothes. It's not as if my classmates routinely set fire to hundred-dollar bills when they were bored. They didn't have to. They just ignored the prices on menus. Money was always there, insulating them, like the soft down in their L.L. Bean quilted vests.

As it happened, my date that night was also passing—as straight. Or maybe he was still figuring out his sexuality. Our common plight would later bring us together. But I am getting ahead of the story.

Talk about insouciance. Young people today have no clue how difficult it was to be homosexual in the 1970s and '80s. I was both envious and aghast recently when the twenty-four-year-old actress Kristen Stewart, unabashedly in a relationship with a woman, refused to identify as lesbian or bisexual. She told *Nylon* magazine, "There are going to be a whole lot more people who don't think it's necessary to figure out if you're gay or straight. It's like, just do your thing."

Do your thing. Jesus. In a mere thirty years, a quirk of biology that had traumatized millions and drove hundreds more to suicide was reduced by this young person to a giant yawn. I remember freaking out in high school when I watched the 1961 adaptation of Lillian Hellman's *The Children's Hour* on late-night TV. In the movie, a malicious child falsely accuses two teachers at a girls' school of being lesbians. No one challenges the child. But the teachers—played by Shirley MacLaine and Audrey Hepburn—are censured. MacLaine's character flips out, then does what lesbians usually did in movies from that era. She hangs herself. Interviewed for the 1995 documentary *The Celluloid Closet,* MacLaine pointed out that the scene would doubtless have sparked protests today. Back then, however, no one questioned it. "Audrey and I didn't even discuss it," Mac-Laine recalled. It was one of those givens. You're a lesbian. You kill yourself.

The poison wasn't just in popular culture. Some bigots tried to use the law against gay people and lesbians. In 1978 a conservative California state legislator championed the Briggs Initiative—a law that would have banned gays, lesbians, and possibly anyone who endorsed gay rights from teaching in California public schools. Blessedly, Californians voted down the law. But it was part of an increasingly paranoid, allegedly religious movement to persecute gay people as they began to get a few basic rights. In 1977 the Dade County Commission in Florida established a law protecting gays from discrimination in hiring and housing. Anita Bryant, a former Miss Oklahoma, Miami resident, and singer with a contract to promote Florida orange juice, reacted with extreme panic to this law. In a 1977 interview with television journalist Barbara Howar, she announced that God had called her personally to stop gays from "recruiting" young people into their way of life. She called her campaign Save Our Children. In the interview, which is available on YouTube, Howar asks Bryant: "Where is your human sense of decency and fairness to people who are different from you?"

Bryant scowls, and returns to her anxiety about children: "Better to burn the school down rather than allow them to be taught by homosexuals."

— — —

The malignant propaganda did its job. Any erotic feelings I might have had for women were suppressed in favor of "appropriate" feelings toward men. Initially, this made for a good time at Yale. Unlike the conformist losers in high school, Ivy League men liked smart women. I liked being liked. My boyfriends opened worlds to me. One brought me into his circle of friends—including Manhattanites whose parents had written books I admired. Another introduced me to opera. Yet another, who worked on *Yale Daily News,* encouraged me to contribute articles and political cartoons to the paper. They were all Jews, and I felt woefully inadequate as a gentile. But my life was on track. Until something as unanticipated as a meteorite collided with it: I fell in love with a woman.

This was awful and wonderful at the same time. Surrendering control terrified me. I thought of her more than I thought of my work. I sketched her face from memory in the margins of my lecture notes. I signed my cartoons with an affected scribble that the legendary cartoonist Pat Oliphant had helped me to design. One night, after she had been working in my room, I found pages of scratch paper on which she had practiced and perfected the scrawl. She and I spent hours talking about writing, which was what we both aspired to do—never mind that my immediate objective involved working as a political cartoonist. For a long time, talking was *all* we did. Because she too was ambitious, and being gay could wreck a career. We apologized if we accidentally brushed against one another. Until a night came when we stopped apologizing.

She was the first woman with whom I had a sexual relationship. I am being deliberately vague about her identity because I fear a nuisance lawsuit from her powerful family. When we finally got together, I had graduated and was living in Manhattan, working at what I thought would be my dream job: political cartoonist for *Newsday*. She had another year in New Haven, during which we continued to see each other. But after her graduation, when the best job offer she received was on the West Coast, we tried to do a damaging, '70s-era thing: maintain our tie to one another while still dating men.

To suggest that this was painful is an understatement. After what struck me as a horrific betrayal, I stopped writing letters and talking to her. Superficial relationships were fine. But I couldn't bear the idea of her having an intellectually intimate relationship with someone—male or female—other than me. To protect myself, I took up with a new man, another writer. Eventually she broke our icy silence, beginning to ease my hurt and enmity. "We need to talk," she told me on the phone, "about what this relationship is—and isn't. And we need to talk in person."

She proposed to fly to New York for my birthday, November 18, and spend the day with me. I was prepared to be let down, brushed off, dumped. I was prepared to be disappointed. But I was not prepared for what actually happened. On November 12, she was killed at point-blank range in a botched mugging. This occurred outside a restaurant in Venice, California, then a run-down neighborhood controlled by street gangs. She was dining with a man who had written her a recommendation for a grant. The news reports—which I could not then bear to read and have only recently found on microfilm—indicated her suffering was brief. Of this I am envious. My suffering, in various permutations, continues to this day.

Many are familiar with Elisabeth Kübler-Ross's five stages of grief: denial, anger, bargaining, depression, and acceptance. I would add: vodka, which tends to supersede the others. Denial was useless. She had bled out in the street. Bargaining too—resurrection was off the table. I didn't feel anger until recently, when I read in the microfilm clips that only one of her two killers expressed remorse.

The thing about having an actual gay relationship when you are gay is that you finally figure out what all the fuss had been about sex. Why the pop songs describe euphoria. What it means to have dopamine overload. How the delicate curve of a lightly freckled nose can set off an explosion of joy. Depression, predictably, made me lose touch with all pleasure. I oozed sadness. It followed me like a snail trail. The Roman Catholic Church, which had previously sustained me, plunged me into self-loathing. I couldn't banish images from *The Children's Hour*. If only she and I had had our talk—and I had gained some resolution, even disappointing resolution. I associated my sexuality with random murder and death. If I had felt myself attracted to a woman in New York, I would have moved to another continent.

I leaned heavily on my gay male friends, including the one who had brought me to the Fence Club dance all those many years ago. I would join them in groups—easily penetrating the velvet ropes of Studio 54 in a cluster of beautiful young men. I sat in the balcony and watched them on the dance floor. I wanted to be loved. I needed to be loved. But I couldn't bear the idea of being touched.

Then one guy—a guy who used his charm like a wrecking ball—broke through. I met my future husband at a bon voyage party given by a crazy person—or, in any event, a meek, unstable copy editor who was winsome when she took her meds and hospitalized against her will when she didn't. She was sailing soon on the *QE2* and wanted to show off the outfits she had bought for the cruise.

The party, as one might have imagined, was filled with "nice" people—people whose sense of self derived from "supporting" those who were not in a position to advance their careers. In those days, newspapers didn't attract nice people. Thus the party was small. The man I had dragooned into accompanying me slipped out after one drink. I found myself pressed into a corner by another young man who did not lack for confidence.

He identified himself as a rare-book and manuscript dealer and began dropping the names of important authors. We swatted pretensions back and forth for a while, and I felt my depression lift. Well, slightly lift. I was drawn to this man's world—a world where one could touch letters written by James Joyce, turn pages of manuscripts by Vladimir Nabokov, caress a volume of Samuel Johnson's *Dictionary*. The young man also looked uncannily like a male version of my dead lover. Something stirred. "What I've been trying to find," I stupidly blurted, "is a first edition of Lewis's *The Apes of God*."

"That's a hard one," he told me. "But I'll do my best." The guests began to depart, and I was among them. The hostess would have no viewers for her cruise wear. Until the young man volunteered to stay. Thoughtful gesture. But I still never expected to hear from him.

The Wednesday after the Saturday of the party, he rang. "I have your book," he said.

I was flustered, audibly broke. "How much will it cost?" I asked.

"I'd love to trade for an original but that's only if you'll have dinner with me on Saturday." We had many more dinners. He brought many more presents, including two signed George Grosz lithographs. I had done my senior thesis on George Grosz. I was falling hard for this man's world. Soon I felt loved. I felt willing to love. And willing to touch.

Nor did I conceal the reason for my grief. He knew, and if it bothered him, he didn't confront me. When I thought of passing as a WASP, I thought of clothes. But I don't remember plotting to wear girly things for my ex-husband. So-called sexy lingerie made me feel foolish. I'd say something hilarious about the getup; he'd laugh, and the mood would die. I owned several Jil Sander pantsuits that telegraphed a certain Germanic androgyny. I cut my hair short. I felt comfortable in the androgynous clothes because I thought they projected my complex identity. Yes, I wore a wedding ring. But I also wore hard, angular black suits and crisp oxfords with heels.

I was deep in the closet when the AIDS epidemic struck. I did not join ACT UP, though many lesbians did. Instead I volunteered to work on the AIDS hotline at St. Clare's Hospital. If I had a dollar for every time I heard the word "fag," I could have retired years ago. I even stumbled on it in my own journal.

I learned to hold my tongue at parties that were given by the demand side of my ex-husband's business. Rich straight men were oddly frightened of the disease; one advocated putting people with HIV in camps. Only once—after way too much champagne—did I lose it, ranting about the way President Reagan refused to use the acronym AIDS until a speech in 1987, more than five years into the epidemic. My hosts rolled their eyes. My ex-husband—who agreed with me in private but not in front of clients—glared. I was not invited back.

To get through these parties, I drank a lot. Possibly too much. So in 1995 I stopped drinking. The official pretext was to get sober so I could get pregnant. But not drinking brought new problems. Without vodka, I noticed things I had previously ignored—artworks with uncertain provenances in our home, for example (a common problem for collectors). In ten years, I had evolved from a twentysomething paralyzed by the murder of her lover. I was stronger, more capable of independence. And without vodka, I wasn't really very heterosexual at all.

In literature, passing often involves short-term gain and long-term regret. You see this in James Weldon Johnson's novel, *The Autobiography of an Ex-Colored Man.* Johnson's character, known only as the "ex-colored man," is a biracial musician in the Reconstruction South. After witnessing a horrific lynching, he decides to pass as white to stay alive, which he does, but at the cost of his dream: making ragtime music. In Virginia Woolf's *Mrs. Dalloway,* the title character swaps passion for passing. Before marrying a man, Clarissa Dalloway loves Sally Seton, with a fervor that only afflicts the very young. It was a passion that, Woolf writes, "could only exist between women, between women grown up . . . the charm was overpowering, to her at least, so that she could remember standing in her bedroom at the top of the house holding the hot-water can in her hands and saying aloud, 'She is beneath this roof . . . She is beneath this roof!'"

I felt these losses—the regrets—of these characters and looked to Alfred Kinsey, the great twentieth-century scholar of sex, for comfort.

Not all things are black, nor all things white. It is a fundamental of taxonomy that nature rarely deals with discrete categories. Only the human mind invents categories and tries to force facts into separated pigeonholes. The living world is a continuum in each and every one of its aspects.

The sooner we learn this concerning sexual behavior, the sooner we shall reach a sound understanding of the realities of sex.

Kinsey understood that sex was a spectrum. I knew I was near the middle of that spectrum. By experimenting with heterosexuality, I was not betraying my tribe. I was expressing a less dominant part of myself. But without vodka, the dominant part was ready to leave her closet.

I fell in love with another woman. My marriage ended, as did the relationship with the woman who had been the catalyst for its demise. I have not chosen partners well in my lesbian career. But I remain hopeful.

Oddly, when I began dating women, I lost interest in androgyny. I felt comfortable looking like a "woman." I didn't fear being identified as the property of a man. Perhaps because I had moved from New York to Los Angeles—a city of glittering surfaces—I pampered myself with regular pedicures and had my toes painted lavender, vermillion, and what a character in Clare Boothe Luce's *The Women* called "Jungle Red." I grew my hair, finally allowing my stylist to do what LA stylists have been called by the universe to do: make their clients ever more blond. Three years ago, after a decade of being out, I was totally comfortable with female drag. On tour for my recent book about Elizabeth Taylor, I indulged in fashions inspired by the star: black cocktail dresses, silk stockings with seams, and the punishing undergarments necessary to sculpt my flesh into Tayloresque curves.

In a recent essay, Gregory Rodriguez described his own insecurity about the identity he projects, and the way random strangers gave him miraculous gifts of reassurance. His essay itself—the acknowledgment of this uncertainty—was a gift to me, because I am often unsure about the identity I project.

Rodriguez described delivering a "nutty" talk at the Getty Museum in LA about the Czech photographer Josef Koudelka, an artist he had never met but "whose stark depictions of exile and alienation" he had admired since college.

Afterward, Rodriguez recalled, Koudelka gave him a present: the artist "asserted rather aggressively in his broken English, 'You are who you are supposed to be. Some people will hate you. Some people will love you. I love you.'"

I dream that a person will one day tell me: "You are who you are supposed to be."

But I don't count on it. As you might imagine, I began this essay in the optimistic summer of 2016, when homophobia really did seem to be in decline. In November of that year, however, the presidential election threw a cruel shadow over my country. The president-elect began assembling a cabinet of bizarre, hate-filled creatures, many of whom endorsed "conversion" therapy for gay people and nearly all of whom favored altering federal law to permit discrimination against the LGBT community for "religious" reasons. The clock was turned back even farther than the 1980s. Forced to endure an increasingly diverse nation, a straight white mob rallied around a strongman, who vowed to restore the soul-devouring conformity of the 1950s.

This strongman did not win the popular vote. Millions demonstrated against him. These millions give me hope. In the 1980s I felt alone. Today I feel part of a proud, self-identified group—facing persecution, yet committed to prevail. No longer shamed into passing. Believing—now more than ever: "You are who you are supposed to be."

On Historical
Passing and Erasure

/ Dolen Perkins-Valdez /

I t is 2015 and I am in Decatur, Georgia, preparing to give
a talk at the Decatur Book Festival. The festival is held in a
beautiful little plaza next to the county courthouse. Festivalgoers
roam the tents, eyeing the copious book displays, clutching their
festival bags. It is Labor Day weekend, and the weather could not
be more perfect: warm with just a hint of coolness in the breeze. I
have a little time before my panel begins, so I too wander a little
aimlessly among the throngs of book lovers.

Given my historical interests, it is inevitable that I eventually
find myself standing in front of the DeKalb County Courthouse,
looking up at a stone statue that resembles the obelisk-shaped
Washington Monument in DC. I know this one is a Confederate monument, but I scrutinize the words etched on the statue
anyway:

ERECTED BY THE MEN AND WOMEN AND CHILDREN OF
DEKALB COUNTY TO THE MEMORY OF THE SOLDIERS AND
SAILORS OF THE CONFEDERACY, OF WHOSE VIRTUES IN

PEACE AND IN WAR WE ARE WITNESSES, TO THE END THAT
JUSTICE MAY BE DONE AND THAT THE TRUTH PERISH NOT.

I have been thinking about the Civil War a lot over the past
few years, thinking of how we memorialize it. I was born and
raised in Tennessee. Long before I developed my acute awareness of history, I rode in the car with my family past the Nathan
Bedford Forrest monument many times on trips between Mem-
phis and Nashville. Perhaps, I'd wondered, there was something
about Forrest besides his involvement with the Ku Klux Klan.
Perhaps there was another, nobler story, unknown to me.

Yet when it comes to Nathan Bedford Forrest, every historical path leads back to the lesser version of the man. Terrorist.
Murderer. There seems to be little that is redeemable in this
man's life, and certainly not enough to memorialize him on a
major interstate highway.

I am intrigued by these revisionist tendencies. As a native
Southerner, literary references to America's relationship with
its past always stand out to me. "The past is never dead. It's
not even past," writes William Faulkner in *Requiem for a Nun*
(1951). In his 1965 essay "White Man's Guilt," James Baldwin
argues, "History, as nearly no one seems to know, is not merely
something to be read. And it does not refer merely, or even prin-
cipally, to the past. On the contrary, the great force of history
comes from the fact that we carry it within us, are unconsciously
controlled by it in many ways, and history is literally *present* in all
that we do." I have begun to think the ahistorical sentiment that
pervades American discourse is not so much a wanton disregard
of history, but more a willful ahistoricism.

There is an impulse in contemporary American culture to
engage in what I prefer to term "historical passing." This is not
so different than racial passing in the years before integration,
when people of color chose to identify as white in order to gain

certain advantages. Likewise, in the twenty-first century, the term *postracial* seeks to move past racial obstacles into a freer, less encumbered world. *Postracial* suggests that race no longer matters, when in fact the failure of the term is its refusal to allow race to continuously evolve in the context of its history. Rather than view race as an in-progress narrative, postracialism seeks to do away with the narrative altogether.

In the post–Civil War years, the desire to pass from blackness into whiteness could be undertaken quite suddenly: a packed bag in the night, a stroke of the pen on a form, an enigmatic response to a question. Contemporary ahistoricism attempts a similarly sudden erasure; for instance, the Fourteenth Amendment is no longer about African American freedmen and -women, it is about immigrants and "anchor babies." By living outside history, we step into a hole that we never even knew existed.

Passing and history are much more entangled than one might imagine. The metaphor of racial passing is inherently inapt—slipping, if you will, into an identity one cannot ontologically claim presupposes a stable definition of identity linked to one's history. What is ethnicity if it is not one's history? Yet anyone who has completed a DNA test with one of the popular ancestry companies understands the difference between science and identity.

The difference, it seems to me, between individual passing and historical passing lies in scale. Self-identification is a form of individual agency, and no one should be denied that right. A national discourse that denies the facts of a country's history presents a much more critical dilemma.

Here is a case in point: Alabama, Arkansas, Georgia, Kentucky, Louisiana, Maryland, Mississippi, Missouri, North Carolina, South Carolina, Tennessee, Texas, and Virginia. These are states with Confederate monuments on courthouse grounds. It is April 2013. I have been following the case of Willie Jerome Manning, who has been on Mississippi's death row for nearly twenty years. I am waiting to hear if the Mississippi State Supreme Court will grant him the right to a DNA test that could exonerate him. In a 5–4 ruling, they refuse. I quickly search online to see if there is a Confederate monument outside the Mississippi State Supreme Court in Jackson. There it is. On the Capitol grounds. State Street, on the south side of the Old Capitol Museum. I feel the weight of history. Confederate monuments in front of state courthouses still feel like a form of terrorism.

In 1871 Liberty, Mississippi, became the first town in the United States to erect a Confederate monument. An ahistorical accounting of that monument might suggest that the year had nothing to do with the Enforcement Act of 1871, which gave the federal government authority to suppress white supremacist organizations such as the Ku Klux Klan. An ahistorical interpretation suggests that Confederate monuments erected on state grounds across the postbellum South have nothing to do with the intimidation of African Americans.

Another case in point. There are various versions of Confederate state holidays in at least nine states. Sometimes this has resulted in an oddly dissonant convergence of narratives. For example, the celebration of Robert E. Lee's birthday on January 19 in Texas sometimes coincides with the celebration of Martin Luther King Jr.'s birthday. Though some might argue that the Lee holiday predates King, the discomfort over this overlap suggests that the continued celebration of Confederate war generals has its issues. This returns me to the words etched on the statue in Decatur: AND THAT THE TRUTH PERISH NOT. I believe we have moved past a debate over the "truth." I am talking about an outright denial of history.

I would like to offer up one more passing metaphor: passing as it relates to death. When we talk about death, we say someone "passed away." In his essay "Of the Passing of the First-Born," W. E. B. Du Bois poignantly moves through a series of emotions:

his initial dismay over his firstborn son being born beneath the shadow of America's racial "veil," his adoration and love for the child, and his despair after the baby's death. Du Bois suggests that this untimely death is a cruel fate for a race that is already so persecuted.

I'm going to say something now that might reveal my Southern penchant for drama. If we pass into an ahistorical space, we engage in a kind of social death as a nation. We seek to destroy our very fabric.

Passing is an act, and to stand outside of American history is an act of imagination. One might argue it is a choice that one has the right to make, but it is a choice nonetheless. Historical passing does not seek to erase all of American history. When one chooses to live outside these historical lines, the boundaries are never fairly drawn. Inevitably, we embrace certain histories and reject others.

I acknowledge the many facets of our history. I know that many of these Confederate monuments were erected long before most of us were born. I know that there are descendants living today of Southern white men who bravely defied their families to follow their conscience and go fight in the Union army. I understand there are many white people who live, work, and raise families in these communities and vehemently disagree with the continued public presence of these monuments. This meditation does not intend to be divisive nor can it be, as there are more sides to the conversation than I or the monuments themselves can adequately represent. Baldwin wrote, "This is the place in which it seems to me most white Americans find themselves. Impaled. They are dimly, or vividly, aware that the history they have fed themselves is mainly a lie, but they do not know how to release themselves from it, and they suffer enormously from the resulting personal incoherence." I wish to impale no one. I merely wish to make visible the many instances of silent historical passing.

It is 2016, and I am finally penning this essay that I have been ruminating over for the last few years. In Washington, DC, my adopted city that I have grown to love, I take the metro and get off at Judiciary Square. I don't come here often, but I know there are many federal and municipal courthouses in this area. I have researched the history of this little section of the city, and I know that it was once a residential neighborhood filled with Italian immigrants. Yet its proximity to the White House and the US Capitol, as well as urban development, ultimately defined its character as more commercial.

I have already seen the statue of Abraham Lincoln nearby. It stands in front of the old DC City Hall, which is now the DC Court of Appeals. It was erected there in 1868. If one knows the history of this statue, one might argue that it was erected in the same era as some of the Confederate memorials and shares a similar desire to wrest control of the narrative. As I mentioned, history has many facets.

Today, I am less interested in the Lincoln Memorial and more interested in a rumor I have heard. There is a statue of a Confederate general, someone has told me, in Judiciary Square. I exit the metro and walk a half block east to Fourth Street before turning south. I check my phone to make sure I am headed in the correct direction. I am a little nervous. Something about Confederate monuments makes me feel like a stranger in my own country.

Once I see the statue, I feel a little foolish for being anxious. The monument is remarkably nondescript. The stately, bearded man is Albert Pike, but he is not dressed in a Confederate uniform. He is dressed in a suit and bow tie and looks more like a distinguished orator than a war general. The words etched on the statue name him a poet and author, with the word *soldier* sandwiched between them. A goddess—I am not sure which goddess—holds a tapestry with the double-headed eagle symbol of the Scottish Rite of Freemasonry. The statue could not be more different than the one of Nathan Bedford Forrest in my home state of Tennessee. In that one, Forrest is riding a horse. His gun is drawn. And he is surrounded by Confederate battle flags. In this one, Pike is a stately freemason.

I look around. The area is flanked by government buildings. A woman in a business suit walks by, talking on her cell phone. Two men don't even glance toward the statue as they chat with one another in front of it. No one even seems to notice Albert Pike is there, let alone that he is a Confederate war general. In fact, the statue itself does not appear to want to elevate his career as a general, instead portraying him as a man of letters. Might one even suggest that the statue is engaged in an act of passing? There I go, being dramatic again.

I enter the metro, thinking of the unruliness of our histories, how entangled we all are. Perhaps even erasure is too simplistic a notion to describe America's relationship with its history. I grab a pole in the train car, stare silently at the many-hued faces around me. Most of us avoid eye contact, but as the train car shakes and rattles to a slow stop between stations I feel a connection with these strangers, a sense that we are all pushing through this journey together.

Stepping on a Star

/ *Gabrielle Bellot* /

The first time a stranger propositioned me as a woman was in a room full of sculptures in a museum. He was a security guard at the National Gallery, far larger and taller than I was, and had waited for the other tourists to leave the room before he began talking to me. At the time, fewer than a handful of people knew I was transgender, and I had traveled to Washington, DC, a place I had never been and had no family in, presenting as a woman. All of my IDs still had an *M* for my sex and an old name that could not have been a woman's, and my voice was still too filled with a deep rumble for anyone not to see I was trans after a few words. I had traveled here so that I could present as a woman for a few days without worrying about anyone I knew running into me—and to see if I could handle myself like this in an unfamiliar city. My plan was to come out as a queer trans woman the following month—and I knew that once I did, once I said those words, like the spell of a witch, I would likely lose the ability to return to my home in the Caribbean.

It was the week of Thanksgiving. Snow had begun to fall. I had walked to the museum in the long black dress, flowing brown coat, and Merlot lipstick of a lonely romantic, and although I knew I could already pass as a cisgender woman visually now if I wore makeup, months before I would begin taking hormones, I had not actually thought that going to the museum would be any different from how it had been in the past as a male. The streets and subway ride from the carnival atmosphere of Union Station had seemed a bit unnerving, but the city seemed relatively empty, and until the guard spoke to me things hadn't really seemed that different.

The guard had seen me eating in the museum café from a distance, but I was so ingenuous at the time that I hadn't taken his glances for more than any other stranger's appraisals. It was only when I ended up in a room of sculptures with the guard again that I truly felt the terror of passing as a trans woman for the first time. He asked me if I was getting "nice" photos with my camera and if I had had a "nice" lunch, smiling widely and using the diminutive words of a casual patronizer. He stepped closer each time he asked me a question. I was so afraid that my voice would give me away that I instinctively began to do something I would regret for many months of harassment later: I smiled back and mumbled rather than ignoring him. Finally the guard came up to me and asked where I was from. I mumbled, "Caribbean." He smiled and nodded, saying, "Yes, yes," and that I was beautiful. Then he grinned and told me to call him soon to have sex with him, his tongue flapping out of his mouth.

I was so scared that I lost my language. "Maybe," I said, afraid a firm no might get him angry. Then I walked away. I almost ran to the second floor. I must have looked like a shipwreck victim, eyes wide and flitting. Here was a man who was supposed to protect me trying to force himself upon me, a narrative I had seen in so many lurid cases of police officers abusing their authority. I imagined telling someone at the front desk, but then I thought of what problems might arise if I did: the way I might not be treated as a woman because my voice would prevent me from passing as one, the way the guard, the authority figure, could perhaps simply deny I was telling the truth, the way pointing him out would likely necessitate coming into contact with him again. I began looking at every male guard, listening to their footsteps. The footfalls most of all. I began learning, without looking, when I was alone in a room—and learning, then, to move on rather than stay by myself. I had begun to learn, essentially, what it is like for so many women, trans or cis, to simply *be* in space, to be aware of where your body is and who is looking at it and who is considering following it. The incident with the guard had been short and quick, but it was one of those small events that felt huge in the moment; later, I wondered if perhaps the guard did not even realize his position of power or how the fact that he had waited until we were alone to speak to me like this might frighten a woman on her own. In the end, I left the museum early, periodically glancing back as I walked through the light snow, hoping I would not see the guard walking after me or hear his footfalls behind me. As small as the event had been, I kept replaying it; the security guard had betrayed me, just as police officers have all too often betrayed young black American men, by removing the illusion that he was just there to protect.

All that afternoon, I tried to quiet the noise in my memories. But I kept hearing that pounding, resounding sound: footfalls, the drum of my heart after I'd fled from the guard.

This was when the idea of passing stepped into my life like a shadow. It happened again almost everywhere I went: With a guard at the Smithsonian American Art Museum, who made me take a photo of him on his own phone and I, too afraid to talk loudly, wordlessly said yes before he tried to ask me to go out with him. And again with a guard in the Peacock Room of the Freer Gallery. It happened with man after man on the streets. It happened with an old Russian taxi driver, who told me, more than once, not to leave his cab because he wanted me; another man had walked me to the Russian's cab, telling the driver, who he must have known, "I have brought you a beautiful girl." I was an object, an objective, and, if they found out I was trans, often objectionable. Once, I looked up at the night sky on my way back from the metro and a thought flitted through me: *This is like living on a new planet.* My female friends had told me stories of being catcalled and stalked before, but I had never understood them until now. Soon, it was just a normal facet of my life, this harassment for being seen as a woman: sometimes comical, sometimes annoying, always a bit unnerving, sometimes terrifying. It became common for men I did not know to speak down to me, often so subtly that I doubted they were aware of doing it. What had seemed so large at first now had become a new norm, yet I still worried each time a man catcalled or propositioned me that I might face violence if he realized I was trans; after all, it is not uncommon for trans women to be assaulted or even killed by someone who reacts in fury to finding out the woman he was flirting with is not cisgender. I was happier than ever, living as a woman, but now I knew more about what womanhood meant.

Passing, suddenly, was always a step behind me.

— — —

I was born an only child in the United States to Dominican parents. At the time, it was not uncommon for Dominicans to try to give their children US citizenship by either having them in America or applying early for US passports, which meant that I, like some of my childhood friends, was fortunate to have dual citizenship—even as my Dominican passport, unable to have its gender or name changed on it, is now an unusable relic. When I was born, my parents had been following their own form of an American dream; as a child, my father had been an island scholar, winning a competitive scholarship that allowed him to leave Dominica to study abroad. But things were still difficult;

not long after my birth, a racist white neighbor came to our driveway one day, called us niggers, and suggested we leave. Beyond the racial unease, my father yearned for the island he and my mother had been born in, and when I was a child we moved back to Dominica, the place where most of my memories begin. I have never felt like an American; Dominica was my family's home, the world that gave me the images and language that would define me as I grew. The island had been named Waitukubuli ("Tall is her body") by the Kalinagos, and our best-known writers were Jean Rhys and Phyllis Shand Allfrey; as a result I found myself on an island that had its words tied mostly to females while I did not feel free to use such language on myself.

Although the compass of all my memories points to my seeing myself as a girl, I did not understand what this really meant for many years. What I remember best was the all-pervading dread of asking my parents to accept behaviors I had been taught did not correspond with my body: wearing makeup around our house, going out in a dress or girls' jeans, calling myself "she." "You are not a girl," my mother would tell me, and I both did and didn't understand what she meant. None of those things, of course, makes anyone a woman or a man. And there is a common misunderstanding among some cis people that binary transgender people simply enjoy conventionally gendered roles, when in fact we see ourselves as *being* women or men in a mind-body sense, unrelated to the objects or behaviors we like—but all the same, I wanted to do the things my female friends and cousins could, yet kept being told this desire was wrong. I struggled with a mind-body problem, albeit one quite different from Descartes'.

I constantly imagined worlds in which I had a female body. So I lived out these fantasies in brief secret moments. I waited for my parents to leave the home on some nights and then sneaked into the little grand palace of my mother's closet, trying on her clothes and makeup and taking photos of myself, the latter a way to make it all seem real and material for a bit longer. I stood on our balcony and gazed at the stars and the vast dark mountains that framed our home and I imagined drifting off on the starship of my dreams, not needing to change when the rumble of my parents' vehicle on the dirt road began and when our German shepherds began to bark. As a young adult I imagined—and still do—having a child; each time I remembered I could never give birth to one, it hurt. I wanted the pains of cis-womanhood too, yet all I had was the pain of believing I could never have it. So I tried to crush the girl inside me, hating her, hating myself because I could not understand why she was there, even as I did. Each time I dated a new girl I dreaded telling them my secret: that I wanted to date them as a woman. It seemed ludicrous to me, like stepping on a star, or expecting the figurehead of a ship to speak. But it was something ludicrous I couldn't get rid of. And, honestly, I didn't know who I would be if I *could* get rid of it. After all, it was me.

Not being able to show love as you are is a kind of living death, a stargazer's blindness.

I never dared present myself as feminine in any way in Dominica. In that island, like much of the Anglo-Caribbean, colonial-era antibuggery laws, along with religious indoctrination, have created an atmosphere in which LGBTQIA individuals are generally neither well understood nor respected if they express themselves openly, and my fear of being labeled gay—a *buller*, a *batty bwoy*, a *boggarah*, the *antiman*, as we called gay and gender-nonconforming men—made me try to suppress the woman inside me for over twenty years. In many ways, passing racially is less complicated in much of the Caribbean than passing as another gender, given the ways that race can sometimes be fluid for us, even as we often cling to old assumptions about the values of whiteness and blackness. I tried to act masculine to throw anyone off my trail; I pretended to be homophobic as late as my early twenties, even as I knew being homophobic and acting masculine felt deeply wrong, even hypocritical. More than once, I considered ending my life.

One memory always returns like the night. I was at college in Florida. I had gone with a kind female friend of mine from Costa Rica back to her dorm, and we were chatting in the kitchen. Suddenly, in walked her roommate with a gay male friend of hers and one of his friends. He was openly gay, and that night he was wearing a belt with rainbow studs, his tight black jeans partly hanging off his ass as he walked, his small gray hoodie slightly coming up above his underwear, showing his skin as he walked. He brought with him the odor of men in gyms and joked about smelling bad as he passed by me. I looked away from him. While everyone chatted with him, I was silent, icy. Later my friend asked me what was wrong.

"I don't like gay people," I told her. "I think it's wrong." Shortly after, I told her, with a kind of unhinged pride, that I was homophobic. It was an outlandish lie. I am pansexual, potentially attracted to anyone on the spectrum of gender. But at the time, I wouldn't admit that. I always remember the way I treated that gay student like the Other, for he represented something that scared me: not that I was a gay male, but that I would be seen as one if I let my sense of womanhood show. And so I Othered him. I Othered myself by Othering the queerness in him. I had left one country for college in another, and even in more liberal America, I was acting the way I had in Dominica. In a silly way, I felt protected from people learning of my transness by these outward displays of homophobia. My self-hatred was a lonely fortress to hide in. Of course, the mirrors in there always showed a woman in love with a woman or, perhaps, with a man. You cannot suppress gender dysphoria, not really. It always came back, always tore down this absurd fortress, making me rebuild it, more laboriously, each time.

Some months before I went to DC, I began presenting as a woman on a trip to London with my best friend in a city where virtually no one knew me. We had traveled together to London for a month to do research in the British Library for the novels we were writing. I hadn't planned to present as female there, but seeing her dress up for nights out inspired me. *Being* a woman is unrelated to clothes or makeup, obviously, but they represented gendered parts of the social constructions of femininity I genuinely enjoyed, just as my friend did. I wanted to be perceived as a woman, like she was, when we went to places: not to cross-dress but to literally be seen as one, in every way. I wasted money on trips on the Tube to get to makeup stores only to walk out of them in fear before any of the employees could talk to me. One day, I decided to be brave and went into a large Boots pharmacy, where a bemused Australian woman suggested products for me to try on at a mirror. The people walking by in the reflection as I tried on nude lipsticks unnerved me, but I persisted, leaving with a bag of mass-produced treasures.

A few days later, my friend asked me in a café in the British Library if my parents knew that I wanted to be a woman. I said that they didn't. She seemed surprised at first, then told me what was obvious: that in this big city, I would have a chance to present as one and see what happened. In some ways, I thought it would be my only chance to do so for a long time, if not forever.

And I began doing so, in small steps, toward the end of the trip. I went to see a play by Derek Walcott, *Omeros*, with a full face of makeup—not particularly well applied makeup, but makeup that made me feel, suddenly, like I was breaking a boundary. I went to the British Library wearing a peacock-blue eyeshadow, at which point an African man who worked behind the desk in one of the rooms refused to help me when I asked him to retrieve a book I had ordered, even though he had assisted me with a smile on the days I had not worn makeup. I walked down Oxford Street and shopped. In the Tube, people stared at me; one sweet person on the train smiled when she sat across from me, then began doing her makeup and glancing at me. Her smile meant the world in that moment: even if I looked a mess, here was someone seemingly smiling in a compassionate, accepting way. A year later, after beginning to transition, I began to appreciate *not* wearing makeup as much as wearing it, and when I was finally able to pass without makeup, I felt a lovely sense of freedom. Makeup, once a partial bridge to a taboo place, had become what it was for so many cis women: an option, not a requirement. These insights mean a lot when you get to learn them later in life, when you blossom as you after a long period of being, in a sense, someone else.

But after the trip ended, I went back to feeling trapped in a place where many people knew me only as male. I felt scared to go out presenting as female. It became agonizing, this sense of entrapment. I came closer than ever before to killing myself, finally, with poison one lurid afternoon when I could no longer take the pretense. I went to see a counselor for the first time soon after, and she helped me see that I could finally be myself by making a plan to come out. When I finally came out to everyone as a queer transgender woman at twenty-seven in Tallahassee, where I was doing my graduate degree, it saved my life—even as it meant giving up something else, for I had already decided, months before I came out, that I would not return to Dominica until I could feel safe there as an openly transgender woman. I was luckier by sheer chance, as a dual citizen; all the same, Dominica was my home, and now I had lost it. My parents themselves told me not to return. I cried many nights at the things my mother said to me, things I knew mothers could say but never imagined mine would: that I would be disowned, that I should forget I had a mother, that I was a failure and an abomination against God, that she herself now felt suicidal. Words thundering in my ears.

I still hear them, sometimes, when the night is too quiet.

— — —

For Seneca, it is possible to turn off noise outside if you can silence it inside yourself. "There can be absolute bedlam without," he wrote in "On Noise," "so long as there is no commotion within." Living as a trans woman, that has become my mantra: to live without screams, inside or out, so I can keep smiling, hoping, dreaming.

It is lovely, sometimes, to turn off the noise. It always shuts off, suddenly, when I am reminded that I am loved by someone else, that the compass of me does not point in all the wrong ways. It is a sudden shock, this silence in the night of the mind. Sometimes, the night is a grand palace, its halls filled with a din of noise, and you just need to find the right door to the right room, where someone you've searched for waits for you under the lamplight, and when you close the door, all the other noise vanishes away.

— — —

The words used to describe passing are not always well defined. We often use words like *white* or *black* or *brown* or *man* or *woman*—all of which have been used, at different times, to describe me—in simplistic ways that assume that all people who we call by such labels will more or less share basic characteristics. Though not a completely absurd assumption on some level, it is too reductive. After all, black can mean many things; one only need read Australian literature to see how the terms *blacks* and *blackfellas* are often applied to Australian Aborigines, like in Patrick White's *Voss*, despite the fact that aboriginal people are often simply left out when people in, say, America use the term *black* as a broad racial term for all persons of a certain darkness of skin. And some South Asians, Polynesians, Maoris, and many other groups have also, of course, been called black or brown in certain contexts; Maori people have even been called Aryans, an extraordinary assertion that derives from the lunatic racialism of a nineteenth-century text called *The Aryan Maori*.

The same is true for simplistic assumptions about gender. If we are going to talk about passing, we need a language for passing—and that language must be precise. I have many problems with the idea of passing, but it is necessary that we talk about it accurately—or, at least, find language that can hold it.

— — —

The night is my translator, the time when language comes to me best.

I like thinking of identity in terms of fields of stars, constellations. For me, it is easy to call one field of stars Woman and another Man, and then, from there, to see how my identity forms a constellation within the field of Woman, even as I have lived before in a different configuration of stars. For some of us, jumping between the fields is simply the norm. Some constellations branch between these two main fields, and others, off in a nearby inky elsewhere, do not really fit within either. There are many constellations in the star fields of Man and Woman; to be a transgender woman is to make up one of the configurations of womanhood, just as tall women and tiny women and women born without uteruses make up their own, even as what my configuration looks like may differ, in its own way, from what another trans woman's looks like, and vice versa. We will not, contrary to certain cis women's fears, erupt into supernovas and destroy the whole field, or turn into black holes and suck everyone into our space. We are women.

I know this, internally, intellectually. But it's easy to forget where you belong in the star fields when you are confronted, day after day, with the fear that you may not pass as a cisgender woman when you enter this restroom or walk down this city block or put on this cut of bathing suit, and you begin to wonder, as you've wondered so often before, if your position in that constellation is precarious. You fear your star will fade and that you will begin to see stars, very different stars, stars that come from a shock to the head, if the wrong person reads you as anything but the cisgender woman they thought you were at first. They will not fade—we are who we are, be we women or men or genderqueer or genderless—but the fear that they might, the fear that lives in the vast shadow of the idea of passing, is one of the most overwhelming I know, a fear that follows some of us down every well-lit hall. In the past I have avoided going to a doctor out of fear that I will not pass and that I will be ridiculed or denied service.

And it can be difficult, though it is necessary, to learn that passing is not our goal if we identify as binary transgender women, as I do. We are women, no matter what we look like, even if not all of us can pass for a woman by the statistical norms of what cisgender females look like. There is nothing inherently wrong with wishing to pass visually, aurally, or otherwise as cisgender; but we do ourselves an intellectual disservice if we fail to realize that the language of passing implies both temporariness and trickery, and aiming to be *recognized* as women, regardless of what we look like, is a much greater goal. And this recognition is not only for others to give us; most of all, it is for you to give to yourself.

It can be a sudden shock, as Virginia Woolf described in *Moments of Being*, to realize that you have accepted yourself as you. That you have come to love yourself. That you have come to learn you would let yourself into your own home if you opened your door at a knock, and found yourself standing before you, a woman without reservations. If I can recognize myself as a woman—well, that's a start to feeling more at home in the field I belong in, to feeling more at home in my language.

Perhaps this is what it means to be a binary trans person: to hear someone say "woman" or "man" and not feel isolated by their words, or even by your own.

— — —

Every time I think I know the language, it becomes bigger, wider, stranger.

Passing is a thing with wings, fins, and ghost-light feet, a thing that follows me everywhere.

I have thought about my ability to pass at seven thousand feet near the open door of a tiny airplane the second time I skydived, wondering if I would pass as a woman in the footage. When I went to Breckenridge by myself to learn how to snowboard, I remember the moment I fell into the snow on my last run down a green slope and hit my shoulder so hard that I was afraid I'd shattered something; I remember my dread not just of possible medical costs, but of the possibility that some bigoted doctor might turn me away if he realized I was trans—for such bigoted doctors, unfortunately, exist. To some cis people, such fears doubtless seem overblown, if not melodramatic. But they aren't hyperbolic, nor the cries of a cult of victimhood. Rather, for many of us, they just describe the contours of our world.

Sometimes, passing makes me feel validated. Sometimes I smile after a man on the sidewalk catcalls me crudely, not because

I like being catcalled but simply because I know someone saw me as an attractive woman. Sometimes the fact that men on online dating sites are shocked that I am trans when I tell them—invariably, they miss it in plain sight on my profile—makes me feel happy. Passing, like prettiness, is a privilege; passing, like prettiness, can also be a peril, if someone believes we are deceiving them.

I remember how I thought of passing the first time I let a man fuck me. How I thought of passing, even though he knew I was trans, had contacted me, indeed, because he wanted an experience with a trans woman. I remember the conflicts: how I wanted to be fucked so badly, yet feared the very thing he wanted from me. How, even though I had invited him into my home, I felt the need to look as feminine as possible when he opened the door, out of the foolish fear that he would flee. And how I felt so happy, finally, when I realized that he wanted me simply for me, not for a version of me that passed, how I felt like a queen stretched out on my bed with him atop me, a queen who was being treated like royalty by this gentle giant of a man, regardless of what genitalia she had or did not. I remember, then, how the noise left my head, and all I felt was joy. Yet even now, so long later, each time I sleep with someone else, man or woman, cis or trans, I think again of how my body passes.

I thought of passing too on the night burglars broke into my apartment, tearing through it like a brief tornado, strewing my clothes and student papers and drawers all over the floor. I had driven home that night with no thought of being burglarized, only to find my window's screen flung onto the grass by my portico, my door left unlocked, my laptops and other electronics stolen. I thought of passing in the terror of opening doors and turning on lights and hoping no one was lying in wait, for I knew that if they thought me a cis woman, they might try to rape me, and if they found out I was not one because I had passed too well on the trips from my home they had perhaps been monitoring from the shadows or if I had not passed and they knew all along I was trans, well, if they knew either way, they might still rape me, but they might also beat the shit out of me not simply for being a woman, but for not being the kind of woman they could believe in, respect enough, if such an absurd term can apply in such a situation, to violate and leave behind without a fractured skull. It can happen to you as a cis woman or a trans woman, this violence, yet as a trans woman who can pass, the specter of punitive violence so often looms larger. I thought of passing when a police officer came to my home and I tried not to let my voice dip down too low, out of fear that he might, as some officers have told trans women in the past, tell me my being so open with such a "lifestyle" had brought this upon me, had made me too visible a target just for being myself.

I was still, even then as the victim of a crime, looking for the language of passing.

— — —

The language is hard to be sure of, but it fills the pages of many books.

Is Don Quixote, lost in the labyrinths of his madness, not attempting to pass as a knight?

Many texts, of course, are explicit in this language. It is hard not to bring up Nella Larsen's 1929 novel, *Passing*, which is one of the most sustained fictional accounts of racial passing, or Mark Twain's *Pudd'nhead Wilson*, in which a white and a "passably" white African American child are switched at birth, with the white child growing up as a Negro servant and the black child being raised as a spoiled white male. The ghosts of passing fill the pages of so many books about American and European fears of miscegenation, like Faulkner's *Absalom, Absalom!* In an essay for *Time* in 1970, prompted by an extraordinary question about what America would look like without black people, Ralph Ellison asserted that America would be inconceivable without blackness, as the country has always been defined by race; in this way, passing is inextricable from defining and conceiving of America, as well.

For obvious reasons, passing also appears in a lot of queer and trans literature, like Kai Cheng Thom's *Fierce Femmes and Notorious Liars*, where the narrator learns, ultimately, that being comfortable as herself is more important than fitting an ideal of cis-normative beauty standards. Trans literature—if broadly defined—also contains some examples of cis characters passing for various reasons as trans, like Ariel Schrag's *Adam*, in which a cis male passes as a trans man, or Rachel Gold's *Just Girls*, in which a cis lesbian takes on the identity of a new transfeminine student to protect the latter from transphobic attacks. Then, there are novels like Bernadine Evaristo's *Mr. Loverman*, in which two gay West Indian men, now living in London, pass as heterosexual married men in order to avoid homophobia, as well as, partly, for the narrator to continue living in denial of embracing his homosexuality.

Perhaps the most interesting texts are ones where passing is less about appearance than behavior. The protagonist of Percival Everett's *Erasure*, an African American writer who writes postmodern novels, is not considered black enough to pass as a "real" African American until he decides to adopt a fictional identity and write a deeply stereotypical novel about life in a ghetto for a black American man. In much colonial literature, like Mulk Raj Anand's *Untouchable*, behavior-based passing becomes a kind of fanatical obsession: the desire to pass not only in terms of race but also in terms of how well one can act like—that is to say, pass as—the colonizing power, or, more broadly, as a social class that is perceived to have more power than one does.

It is difficult, too, to forget the complex historical realities of passing in events like the Parsley Massacre of 1937, in which the Dominican Republic's dictator, Trujillo, ordered the death of vast numbers of Haitians then living on the borders of the Dominican Republic. During the lead-up to this horror, Afro-Haitians were, according to a legendary order from Trujillo, distinguished from Afro-Dominicans by how they pronounced the word *perejil* (parsley), with those able to pass by pronouncing the word like the Dominicans having a greater chance of escaping. Passing, here, becomes woven to pronunciation, race and language braided into the so-often-salvific illusion-reality of being able to present, convincingly enough to the judge, as the expected thing. For the great cartoonist George Herriman, a part-black Creole who created *Krazy Kat*, passing as white—or, at least, sowing enough confusion about his ancestry to make those around him assume he *wasn't* black—was a critical career move; Herriman may well have lost his job under William Randolph Hearst had he been outed as black. *Krazy Kat*, a grand modernist strip in which both gender and race are sometimes fluid, owes its existence to passing—and, poignant as it is, it is unlikely Herriman would have created the same strip had his own internal landscape not been defined by the struggles of racial identity.

Texts and events like these show how passing is often not only about how you look but how you act—something binary trans individuals perhaps know best of all.

Of course, speaking of passing is not necessarily the same as speaking of being, authentically, what we are. When I say I am transgender, this is not a whimsical choice. All humans have a gender identity—a sense of how our body and mind connect to each other in terms of maleness or femaleness. Most people do not think of these things, since they have no need to; their gender identity, like their sexual orientation if they are straight, is just something in the background, never in need of explanation or examination. But for those of us who are transgender, our gender identity often conflicts at some level with our bodies, and so what should have been something negligible in the background becomes part of our foreground. This is something that, as with sexual orientation, science is slowly coming to better understand, through genetics, epigenetics, endocrinology, and neuroscience. Sexual orientation and gender identity, while different, are also similar; both are just there, things we just have, that most of us never need to think about, unless there is some conflict in our body or in how our identities relate to the norms of the society we live in.

Ultimately, humanity is complex, Sphinxian, strange. And I like it being complex. I like people living their lives as whatever makes them feel happiest, if it does not harm anyone else. I do not wish to hate, even if I too must remind myself of it when faced with people who seem disgusted by me simply being me. Hatred, after all, is not so much a failure to love as a failure to try to understand complexity or difference. And we can all be better, in a small yet big way, by understanding that.

— — —

Sometimes we *want* to pass as different things in different places.

I know it well, this desire to emphasize one space on the map of myself over another. In America, I often want my Caribbeanness to be clear; I don't want to feel like I've lost a part of me through living somewhere else. In Dominica as a young adult, I sometimes felt distant from the island and yearned to be back in America, for there is a claustrophobia in knowing you will be called "American" by many Dominicans for listening to rock, for skateboarding, for being an atheist, and even, if you are not beaten up, for being queer. I have been called "white" in Dominica as a result of my interests and the lightness of my skin, yet I invariably become "black" or, most frequently, that catch-all term *Hispanic,* when I enter the United States, based on my appearance: my olive-brown skin, my tight corkscrew curls of black hair, my full lips. Shortly after 9/11, a TSA official once even told me I looked like "an Arab" and gave my carry-on additional screening. Since I have never seen myself as white and cannot pass as white in a white-majority country, I am glad to not be seen as such—but I am always awaiting definition, it seems, due to my ethnic ambiguity.

I am multiracial, ultimately; I inescapably fit into multiple fields along the lines of race because I am perceived as multiple things. I am most accustomed, however, to simply being what we call *shabine* in Dominica, St. Lucia, and other islands in the archipelago, a mixed-race person with light skin, a figure perhaps most memorably defined in a poem of Derek Walcott's, "The Schooner *Flight*." For reasons that likely intersect with colonial notions about white skin equaling wealth and higher value than darker skin in many of our islands, *shabines* are frequently portrayed as the most desirable. The shabine cannot really pass as white or black by appearance, yet can pass as either more abstractly: as "white" in terms of societal privilege, and "black" in terms of being accepted as nonwhite by other nonwhite persons.

The shabine represents the binary of whiteness and blackness—and anyone who believes we have abandoned casual racism in our islands, or outside of them, is severely misinformed.

— — —

The first time my mother referred to me as her daughter was at a concert in Tallahassee. We were sitting at the back of the Ruby Diamond auditorium in the intermission, and the couple in front us had stood up to stretch their legs. My father struck up a conversation with the man about the brilliance of the cellos. In a moment, we were all speaking to each other. After a while, the man introduced himself and his wife. I hesitated.

I had come out to them two years before. I had seen them in person a few times since, but only outside of Dominica. This time, they had come up for medical appointments, as they could find better treatments in the United States than in our island.

I was in a blue dress. They had become accustomed to seeing me like this. My father had come around first, offering his support to my transition, but he still struggled with using my new name and pronouns because the old ones were rooted so deep in his memories. My mother, I knew, loved me, yet my transition still hurt her. Even as she sat next to me, she seemed far away, as if her body was here but her mind was elsewhere, hidden away in a little igloo. I loved them so much, yet no one had made me cry as much as they had over my transition. And yet they had helped me grow too, by seeing how much they were struggling; we had all hurt each other, often perhaps without meaning to, but at least we were here, together, in a place filled with the right kind of noise.

"And this is my daughter, Gabrielle."

I was so happy I almost began to cry. Acceptance does not mean that all is well—I still can't return home without putting myself or even my parents in potential danger. And my mother would still tell me, after this, that she wanted her son back, that I needed to return to God and maleness alike, that I was setting myself up for a life of misery because, to her, queerness was the same as incomprehensibility, as failure, as stepping on a burning star with arms outstretched. I learned to dread calling my parents simply out of the fear that my new voice—the one that I trained to have a new resonance and pitch, as hormone therapy for trans women has no effect on our voices if we begin transition after puberty—would sadden them more, as my mother had told me one day, on the verge of tears, that I no longer looked or sounded like the child she had raised. Acceptance, like rejection, is not always absolute. But we grow as we learn more. We become bigger as our capacity for love does, even if our steps are small.

I often wanted to quiet the noise in my head of footfalls, furious words from my mother, crass catcalls. But this time, as my mother and father said those words, I wanted to hear them forever.

Sometimes it is petrifying, the way it feels that if I do not pass, I will pass, instead, into the undiscovered country, like so many trans women of color before me, if the wrong person reads the book of my being. Too many trans women see Lady Death in the mirror rather than themselves. But it feels right to be myself. And I wouldn't give that up for all the wishes a genie could grant, even if that genie could rewrite my past so I had been born as a cis woman. I would not have been me, really, had I been born cisgender. As we travel, after all, our past changes, as we do in the present; the traveler into the future leaves behind a wake of self as tenuous as seafoam. And perhaps nothing reveals this better than transition. I've felt pain—but that makes the joy of womanhood even more meaningful to me now than if I had always known it from the start.

We cannot stop talking about passing. It is part of our past, present, future. But we should stop talking about it as if it is an ideal, or as if it is merely an ignorant form of idealization. It is both, and it is neither; it is too complex to be so constrained. I wish to be recognized as a multiracial woman, but recognition is a privilege, not a guarantee. I wish to work toward a world in which we can recognize people for who they truly are, but that is not a world in which passing will cease to exist, for passing is too ingrained in too many layers of history and culture. And the best we can do is to understand the nuances and importance of the language we use in each and every context, so that we do not uphold old supremacies—racial, sexual, gender-based—while merely adjusting the words we use.

On most days, I just want to be able to point to my constellation and think, *Yes, that's me*, without hearing any footfalls, any noise, nothing but me and the marvelous mundane calm of recognizing myself for me.

Perhaps love and recognition share the same mirror.

Class Acts

Ways to Be Something You're Not

/ *Clarence Page* /

We have to dare to be ourselves,
however frightening or strange
that self may prove to be.

—MAY SARTON

"**Y**ou may not have a dime, but always *look* prosperous," Grandma Page used to say. Looking back, I realize how surprisingly valuable her advice turned out to be. There's something about looking as though you have money, it seems, that makes people more willing to give you money.

"Son, just prepare yourself," she would say on other occasions, "for the doors of opportunity are opening up and when they do you must be ready to step inside." Little did she know just how prescient she was. It was 1965. The Civil Rights Act of 1964 had passed. The Watts riots were about to happen that summer. Riots would open doors to the white-owned major media for aspiring nonwhite journalists like me. Editors and news directors looked around their newsrooms and realized a need. They could use a few reporters and photographers who could be sent out to "the ghetto" and pass, without looking too conspicuous.

I was about to head off to college, a big deal for a black working-class kid in a southern Ohio factory town like mine. The passing of time has revealed to me how fortunate I was. Small-town life in the 1950s and '60s was a crushing bore for a restless and hyperactive youth like me. But I learned the value of the now well-known old African saying that it takes a village to raise a child. In our little town, Middletown, Ohio, I had a conservative Baptist church to give me some discipline, lots of dramatic Bible stories and cool gospel tunes beginning at age three. I had the Boy Scouts to teach me some table manners at summer camp. (One hand in your lap, the other holding your eating utensil. No elbows on the table.) I had theater, debate, a student newspaper and yearbook to teach me to collaborate with others and *e-nun-ci-ate clear-ly.*

Thanks to decent grades and a mother who wanted to slip her son in to rub elbows with the black aristocracy, I even had a debutante ball, the Cincinnati Links cotillion, to attend as escort to one of the most popular girls in our high school. Her regular boyfriend didn't want to rent a tux, attend rehearsals, or take ballroom dancing lessons so, *blam!* Clarence to the rescue!

The Links is one of the most prestigious national sororities in black America. Since my parents were not doctors or lawyers but a factory worker (Dad) and a professional cook (Mom), this was a rare opportunity for me to associate with black America's upper crust. It also enabled me to pick up some rare insights about class in America, a country that prides itself on not caring about class, even though we're profoundly invested in it.

As I would later read in E. Franklin Frazier's classic study *Black Bourgeoisie* (1957), fancy sororities and fraternities grew out of African American accommodations to new conditions in the Americas. Frazier raised a lot of hackles in the black middle and professional class with his candor, particularly about middle-class African Americans embracing a subservient conservatism. Yet Frazier stood by his argument that the black middle class was marked by conspicuous consumption, wish fulfillment, and a world of make-believe. That's because, for all of their big cars, fine homes, and beautiful clothes, the black bourgeoisie lacked a true *leisure class* to match that of the white aristocracy and their trust fund babies. The black bourgeoisie, as Franklin put it, "still work for a living."

"The rich are different from you and me," F. Scott Fitzgerald is said to have said.

To which Ernest Hemingway is said to have responded, "Yes, they have more money."

In that spirit, I said to my young self as I basked in the ballroom splendor of my fellow debutantes and escorts, we're all passing now. The black bourgeoisie was a lot like me, passing for rich, except they had a lot more money. Being in their proximity helped me as much as the Scouts did to fulfill my grandma's advice: they modeled how to keep elbows off the table and at least *look* prosperous.

For me this was an early lesson in the value of passing. Each of us has two identities: the one that we know ourselves to be and the one that others see when they interact with us. "Passing" is the label that we give to the practice of changing our public identity without, one hopes, losing track of who we truly are. I could not pass for white, but with a nod to Grandma's wisdom I often have tried to pass for rich. I know I have succeeded too well when people turn to me for, say, large charitable donations. My Brooks Brothers suits are bought on sale. My budget is closer to working stiff than donor class.

While there are myriad ways to pass, I'm intrigued by economic passing, the act of leading others to believe you belong to

a higher—or lower—economic class or social status than the one
to which you actually belong.

In this category I include the ambitious climbers in the model
of Fitzgerald's Jay Gatsby. The former Jimmy Gatz hustles his
way up the economic ladder to ostentatious wealth, yet falls short
of cracking the *class* ceiling that separates him from true aristocracy and the love of his life, Daisy Buchanan.

I also include the one-downsmanship of populist "poverty
snobs." They applaud their neighbors who move up and away,
as long as they don't forget where they came from or give even
a hint that they think they're better than those whom they have
left behind.

I see passing of various types in every race and stratum of our
society. Deceptions, big and small, are inevitable in a society that
simultaneously romanticizes both upward mobility and contra-
dictorily the national myth of a classless society, even as everyone
knows full well that the myth is just that, a myth.

In a society like ours with porous class ceilings and boundless
ambitions, it is not unfair to say that passing is the American Way,
whether we can talk openly about it or not. We are a nation of
passers and simultaneously a nation in denial about class. When
people say they have no "class" in their town, they mean no class
warfare. The best way to avoid class warfare, in the denialists'
way of thinking, is to avoid talking about class. Many who are
quite comfortable with talk about race, sex, religion, or venereal
diseases will clear the room before engaging in a frank discussion
of class.

Poverty snobs.

Yet even if we don't want to deal with class in America, it will
find ways of dealing with us. For perspective, it helped me to read
the 2016 best seller *Hillbilly Elegy: A Memoir of a Family and a
Culture in Crisis,* by J. D. Vance, a writer-lawyer who has a lot
in common with me except for age and race. We both grew up

in Middletown, Ohio, although about thirty years apart. I grew up there when the town was on its way up—or so we thought—thriving with steel mills and paper mills in robust post–World War II prosperity. Vance grew up when the town was on its way down, along with every other Rust Belt factory town whose jobs moved overseas beginning in the 1970s.

Vance grew up in cleaner air than I did but also with substantially fewer jobs and a great deal more family dysfunction. The old neighborhoods we knew now struggle against decay. In 2014, deaths by drug overdoses in the county where we grew up began to outnumber deaths by natural causes, according to the coroner's office.

But despite a lot of family and community problems in his upbringing in Middletown and Kentucky, Vance joined the Marines and graduated not only from Ohio State but also from Yale Law School in a coming-of-age drama with which mine cannot compete. Some of his most amusing adventures, now that he has survived them, came with his efforts to adjust to the New Haven world of academic elites. Not an easy task, as I can attest, for kids whose definition of a fancy night out means dinner at Cracker Barrel or another franchise that offers free breadsticks.

You would need a heart of stone to feel anything but sorry for him at a high-stakes dinner where a prestigious law firm scouts for rising talent at one of New Haven's fanciest restaurants:

> The rumor mill informed me that the dinner was a kind of intermediate interview: We needed to be funny, charming, and engaging, or we'd never be invited to the DC or New York offices for final interviews. When I arrived at the restaurant, I thought it a pity that the most expensive meal I'd ever eaten would take place in such a high-stakes environment. Before dinner, we were all corralled into a private banquet room for wine and conversation. Women a decade

older than I was carried around wine bottles wrapped in beautiful linens, asking every few minutes whether I wanted a new glass of wine or a refill on the old one. At first I was too nervous to drink. But I finally mustered the courage to answer yes when someone asked whether I'd like some wine and, if so, what kind.

"I'll take white," I said, which I thought would settle the matter. "Would you like sauvignon blanc or chardonnay?" I thought she was screwing with me. But I used my powers of deduction to determine that those were two separate kinds of white wine. So I ordered a chardonnay, not because I didn't know what sauvignon blanc was (though I didn't) but because it was easier to pronounce. I had just dodged my first bullet. The night, however, was young.

I sympathize. I too had to learn that there is more to ordering wine than white zinfandel or Liebfraumilch. I didn't need to learn all of the labels, just enough to pass.

BEHIND THE MASK

"Masking" is a particular kind of passing, one in which you don't alter all of your identity, only what others perceive to be your attitude.

The label is, of course, inspired by Paul Laurence Dunbar's poem "We Wear the Mask." Dunbar (1872–1906) is widely remembered as the first African American poet to receive global attention. But back in his hometown, Dayton, Ohio, near where I grew up, he was known by many as the "elevator poet," because he would sell his poetry while working as a four-dollar-a-week elevator operator at a downtown hotel. This was the best job he could find as a black man. Fortunately Dunbar's poems sold briskly enough for him to make back his investment quickly. He also attracted the attention of James Whitcomb Riley, the popular Indiana "Hoosier Poet," and others who helped Dunbar gain international attention.

"We Wear the Mask" may be his most famous poem and is certainly my favorite for its irony-loaded imagery of a servant pretending to be content with his life's daily humiliations. It expresses an attitude appropriate to its times, the 1890s. Reconstruction had ended. Union troops had pulled out. Lynchings, disenfranchisement, Ku Klux Klan terrorism, and Jim Crow racial segregation had become the law of the land in the South and in parts of the North too.

All of which left black Americans feeling angry, betrayed, and resentful, but only from behind a safe and false face that "grins and lies."

We wear the mask that grins and lies,
It hides our cheeks and shades our eyes,—
This debt we pay to human guile;
With torn and bleeding hearts we smile,
And mouth with myriad subtleties.

Why should the world be over-wise,
In counting all our tears and sighs?
Nay, let them only see us, while

We wear the mask.
We smile, but, O great Christ, our cries
To thee from tortured souls arise.
We sing, but oh the clay is vile
Beneath our feet, and long the mile;
But let the world dream otherwise,
We wear the mask!

The poem resonates powerfully with me. Every time I hear it I am reminded of every subservient job I ever have had, including my two years in the US Army. It resonates with me as the national anthem of racial and social passing. It is a proper anthem today, as it was in 1895, for a servant underclass. It is not hard to imagine Dunbar composing it in his mind as he rode his elevator up and down with the hotel's elites. I am sure that he heard many things from his passengers. But it is not hard to imagine that all saw one of only two faces: happy or passive. Never angry. After all, he wore the mask expertly.

— — —

I am not alone in believing that, once you dig down, race in our politics and social policy is only the most visible marker for deeper problems related to socioeconomic class. But we don't often use the language of passing to discuss those who bypass barriers of class, partly because Americans always have been quite ambivalent about whether we even have classes.

"We have right on this street every class," a Chicago woman described her neighborhood to Studs Terkel in his *Division Street: America* (1967). "But I shouldn't say class because we don't live in a nation of classes." Instead, she describes the population in her neighborhood through occupations. "But we have janitors living on the street," she said, "we have doctors, we have businessmen, CPAs."

Sociologists have long dealt with the challenges of being told that "there are no social classes in the place where the interviewee lives," wrote Paul Fussell in his *Class: A Guide Through the American Status System* (1983). "Actually," Fussell observed, "you reveal a great deal about your social class by the annoyance or fury you feel when the subject is brought up." For example, he observed, a tendency to get very anxious suggests that "you are middle-class and nervous about slipping down a rung or two." Upper-class people, by contrast, seem to enjoy the topic because it makes their own good fortune sound even more fortunate. Working-class folks don't seem to mind talking about their class identity, either, Fussell said, because they know they can't do much to change it.

— — —

Class passing, not surprisingly, can take multiple forms. We have blacks who pass for white and, in rare cases like Rachel Dolezal, whites who pass for black. We have black and white Americans who boast of having Native American Indian blood, although in many cases including my own family and, more famously, that of Senator Elizabeth Warren, the actual evidence is lacking. As the late Vine Deloria Jr., author of *Custer Died for Your Sins: An Indian Manifesto* (1969), noted with sarcastic irony, Indians are the minority that almost every American wants to claim in their family tree—as if that drop of Indian blood makes them just that much more American than most other Americans.

Our American melting pot has become a gumbo, a collection of meats, vegetables, and spices that give flavor to the pot and absorb flavor from it. Yet the elements in the pot do not completely melt. They maintain their identity. It's the flavor of it all that by its very dynamism defines American culture through war and peace *e pluribus unum*—out of many, one.

For centuries we have had gays who pass for straight and transgenders who pass for cisgender. There's my grandma's everyday assimilate-for-success spirit, a spirit embodied in the slogan of some Jewish executives in the *Mad Men* era: "Dress British, think Yiddish."

There are the bold striver realists who burst through class ceilings to reach for the American Dream by any means that they can get away with—symbolized by F. Scott Fitzgerald's Jimmy Gatz, who hustled his way up to become the title character in *The Great Gatsby*.

And there are the other strivers who, even as they make it up the ladder, do all they can to publicly pass for "po'"—which my factory-worker father used to define as "so poor we couldn't afford the *o* or the *r*"—to avoid one of the biggest social sins an American can commit: acting like you think you're "better than everybody else."

The notion that class and race are the same has been around for a long time. It emerged from the same thinking that gave us "blue blood" as slang for nobility, after the medieval belief that the blood of nobles was blue, different from the rest of us humans. Even the United States; with all the Enlightenment principles on which our country was founded, Americans couldn't help but cobble together an aristocracy of our own, standing firmly against incursions by the nouveau riche.

Although one can find many Jay Gatsbys in American literature and pop culture, today's most instructive example is probably Don Draper, the enigmatic advertising executive portrayed by John Hamm at the center of AMC's *Mad Men*. As we discover early in the series, Draper has risen to prize-winning prominence in his industry while living a lie.

"Draper? Who knows anything about that guy?" says one of his colleagues. "No one's ever lifted that rock. He could be Batman for all we know."

Actually, Donald Francis Draper is revealed to be Richard "Dick" Whitman, born in rural poverty to an Illinois prostitute who died in labor and an abusive alcoholic father who dies after a spooked horse kicks him in the face—in front of ten-year-old Dick. He winds up with relatives who run a bordello. Years later, he goes off to the Korean War and, in a life-changing moment, decides to steal the identity of a fallen comrade.

Many see Draper as a man who has reinvented himself. I see a man who is passing.

He might as well be black, I thought as these scenes unfolded before me, except that if he had been black in 1950s New York, there was no way he would be hired by a Madison Avenue ad firm except maybe as a janitor.

As a cynical critique of the America Dream myth, Don Draper dramatizes the mixture of ambition and caution shared by many of us who, with a mixture of luck, cleverness, and perseverance, managed to work our way up from working-class poverty to the middle class.

Whitman/Draper lives a warped version of the American Dream in the waning days of 1950s class-consciousness. Like Jimmy Gatz, he faced the unfairness of a hardscrabble life that seemed to be rigged against him and found shortcuts around anything that got in his way, including some laws. In keeping with the traditional "passing" narrative, Whitman and Gatz know that life is not fair. Sometimes you have to cut corners just to give your merit a chance to show itself.

THE *DUCK DYNASTY* CANARD

With their waist-length ZZ Top beards, camo-colored outdoors-man clothes, and bayou drawls, the Robertson family men on A&E's *Duck Dynasty* are rustic bumpkins who make *The Dukes of Hazzard* look like *Suits*. So imagine my surprise to learn that Phil Robertson, the grumpy big-bearded grandpa who looks like he came out of Dogpatch, holds two college degrees in education.

And his long-bearded son Willie, famous for his stars-and-stripes bandana, holds a bachelor's degree in business from the University of Louisiana at Monroe. He gets most of the credit for growing Duck Commander from a top-selling duck call invented by his dad into a multimillion-dollar hunting gear enterprise— and TV show—based in Louisiana.

All it took to blow their cover was a Google Images search of the "Duck Dynasty Robertsons" and . . . *blam!* Old family snapshots popped up circa 2000 of Phil and "the boys" smiling at the camera in khakis and sport shirts and *clean-shaven*, which made them all look like the reunited Beach Boys off on a golfing afternoon.

Sure I know that so-called reality TV shows create their own reality. But I still felt punked. My mistake was to allow myself to be seduced by the program's humor and down-home warmth. I wanted it to be real, which is precisely the reaction that the People Who Make TV want me to feel.

Their image of Louisiana swamp-dog authenticity helped their so-called television show rocket to the top of what has variously been called (trigger warning: derogatory slang about poor white people dead ahead) "hillbilly chic," "redneck chic," and "white trash chic."

It is perhaps only coincidental that shortly after Barack Obama's election in 2008 a new bumper crop of TV shows blossomed on the airwaves out of the world of low-income white folks. *Duck Dynasty* appeared along with such other titles as *Swamp People*, *Here Comes Honey Boo Boo*, *Hillbilly Handfishin'*, *Redneck Island*, *Moonshiners*, and *Appalachian Outlaws*. Before rural and small-town America virtually carried President Donald Trump to the White House, it boosted the bayou-based Robertson family of *Duck Dynasty* into superstar status as folk heroes. In 2013 the show's fourth season premiere drew 11.8 million viewers; the most-watched nonfiction cable series in history, according to *E!* online.

For legions of devoted viewers, "these duck-hunters-turned-millionaires are the new faces of the American Dream," said *Forbes* at the time. "And boy, do their faces move merchandise." *Duck Dynasty* product tie-ins had raked in no less than $400 million in revenues, according to *Forbes*, with branded merchandise in Walmart, Target, and Kohl's taking up entire aisles in some stores. Casual camouflage clothes, stars-and-stripes bandanas,

REAL WOMEN DRINK BEER glasses, HAPPY HAPPY HAPPY stickers, STING LIKE A BUTTERFLY, PUNCH LIKE A FLEA T-shirts and other merchandising flew off the shelves.

Yet, as with most other reality TV, the reality of *Duck Dynasty* was heavily manipulated, often to the consternation of the top duck. In one 2012 interview with *Sports Spectrum*, a Christian sports publication, Grandpa Phil fumed that editors on the show had asked the family to avoid saying the name of Jesus during the dinner prayers that were a standard feature of the end of each show. The prayers were being censored, Roberson said, to avoid offending non-Christians.

Show producers also had added *bleep* sounds at random moments of dialogue, Robertson complained, as if to cover up a profanity even though none had been spoken. Judging by Grandpa Phil's remarks, it was not enough that the father and brothers look stereotypically poor; they had to sound like it too.

In other words, the Robertsons were *passing for poor*—and that's just the way their fans love them. The secret, family members say, is that they're a family who love each other and enjoy each other's company—and how that's more important than wealth.

As much as our cultural folklore is filled with rags-to-riches stories, we spend almost no time talking about the flip side: passing for poor. Yet, just as those who fail to raise a finger to improve their economic status draw our contempt, so do those who make it up the ladder and thumb their noses at those whom they have left behind. You can be rich, but don't be uppity about it. Sarah Palin comes to mind.

THE PRISONER OF WHARTON

Race aside, people pass for all sorts of things—richer, poorer, or more or less "regular guy" or "ordinary person" than they really are—depending on what they think will connect best with others.

This is particularly true of politicians seeking to connect with voters. Which leads me to consider a certain New York billionaire, reality TV host and, oh, yes, president of the United States.

Donald Trump claimed a net worth of more than $10 billion and an income of $557 million during his 2016 presidential campaign. But *Forbes*, *Politico*, and the *Wall Street Journal* reported that his net worth and income were considerably less. He's still rich, they said, but not that rich.

Based on his disclosures, *Forbes* estimated that Trump was worth only about $4.5 billion while *Bloomberg* estimated $2.9 billion. As *Politico* said, he appeared to arrive at his figures by overvaluing his properties, ignoring his expenses, and, unlike every other presidential candidate in recent decades, refusing to release his income tax returns.

It does not sound coincidental, then, that nothing seems to infuriate Trump more than allegations that he is not as wealthy or intelligent as he says he is. "I think you're trying to make me as poor as possible," he told *Forbes* in October 2015.

Even when he agreed to be roasted by Comedy Central in 2011, writer and performer Anthony Jeselnik told Joan Rivers in a 2013 interview, Trump told the hosts they could joke about anything, except one: they couldn't say Trump had less money than he claimed to have.

Jeselnik thought Trump's choice was curious. He was more accustomed to other such roast targets as Rivers and David Hasselhoff, who requested that the comedians lay off their children.

"Donald Trump's rule was, don't say I have less money than I say I do," he says in a clip from the show posted online by *Mediaite*. "Make fun of my kids, do whatever you want, just don't say I don't have that much money."

Why is the motormouthed billionaire so closed-mouthed about his own finances?

Financial journalists and other experts speculate several reasons. For one, since Trump's most lucrative business appeared to be the selling, renting, and leveraging of his own brand, it benefits him to fool all of us into accepting the highest number possible.

Two, he also may have been paying such a low tax rate that it would have embarrassed him in front of his supporters.

Three, his businesses appeared to be generating more revenue than cash for him. He was selling assets and increasing debt in the summer of 2016 in ways that suggest a man scrambling for ready cash, *Politico* reported.

Even more intriguing than Trump's unverifiable wealth estimates is his record of fibbing about his own lineage.

For years Trump told people that he was of Swedish descent and repeated that claim in his autobiography, *The Art of the Deal*, according to Timothy L. O'Brien, executive editor of *Bloomberg Gadfly* and author of *TrumpNation: The Art of Being the Donald*.

In fact, Trump is of German descent. His family's original name was Drumpf. Why the switch? As Trump family spokesmen told reporters, they feared that their German heritage would offend Jewish tenants in their buildings.

— — —

As a presidential candidate, Donald Trump managed to play both ends of the passing game. With the salesmanship of a born hustler, he disrupted his own billionaire narrative to voice the attitude and monosyllabic vocabulary of a working-class hero.

On the other end, he repeatedly mentioned his diploma from the University of Pennsylvania's prestigious business school Wharton, as if he still needed academic evidence that he was worth listening to—and voting for.

In fact, after transferring from Fordham University, the future president only spent his final two college years in Wharton's *undergraduate* program, not in the graduate school for which Wharton is best known.

And, contrary to claims in profiles published in the 1970s and '80s that Trump graduated number one in his Ivy League class, the *New York Daily News* interviewed his classmates and found there was no official ranking. "If he tries to claim he was first in the class," the newspaper quoted one student as saying, "he should show his transcript." He didn't.

Candidate Trump kept a tight grip on information about his wealth too, including his tax returns, which he refused to make public, unlike other presidential nominees.

Yet, as bizarre as such disputes and secrecy seem when compared to other more traditional candidates, Trump's core supporters stayed remarkably loyal, understanding perhaps that hype-fueled reinvention is indeed the American way.

We are long accustomed to politicians who brag about their poor-but-character-building childhoods (Abe Lincoln's log cabin anyone?) or who make light of their wealth.

"Poverty snob" was the label my late wife had for people such as herself, fiercely convinced that their tough upbringing made them better people than those of us who didn't have it quite as rough. But reverse snobbery also describes Trump's populist pitch when he's reaching out to his working- and middle-class base of voters who feel put upon by what he calls our "*stoo-pid* leaders in Washington."

"He had one of those rare smiles with a quality of eternal reassurance in it, that you may come across four or five times in life," wrote Fitzgerald. "It faced, or seemed to face, the whole external world for an instant and then concentrated on you with an irresistible prejudice in your favor. It understood you just as far as you wanted to be understood, believed in you as you would like to believe in yourself."

Fitzgerald was writing about Gatsby, but he could have been describing Draper. Or Trump.

DAYS OF FUTURE PASSING

When I think about the future of passing, a classic *New Yorker* cartoon comes to mind. It shows a dog tapping out a message on a computer screen: "On the Internet, no one can tell you're a dog."

When web surfing dogs don't sound all that extraordinary, what else is left in future technology to amaze us? On the Internet it is easier than ever to follow Grandma Page's edict: always look prosperous. You can look any way you want to. Exotic identity shifts are even encouraged. You can produce avatars of yourself that may be of another color or gender or species. You too can be a purple Vulcan.

Through your avatar you can even date other avatars on platforms like Second Life and Utherverse. Real world marriages have been known to break up under the pressure of competition from online relationships that don't rely on traditional standards of appearance or presentation.

Traditional standards are changing on all fronts. I have a theory that changing times will bring more passing by class. Just as the original Gatsby came out of an industrial age ethos that tried to reward cleverness and ambition regardless of blue blood or its lack, today's Gatsby is more likely to come out of a postindustrial meritocracy that can't quite live up to its meritocratic promise. We say we want merit, talent, and intelligence regardless of race, creed, color, or family wealth. Yet there always will be those who turn to deceptions, whether mild or major, in the hope that somebody will give them a pass. After all, passing is the American way.

Jewess in
Wool Clothing

/ Susan Golomb /

When I was married and my then husband and I visited Ireland, where half of his ancestors are from, everyone we met thought that I was the one who was looking for her roots. This thrilled me for reasons I'm not sure of. Was the actress in me proud of how well I could lose myself in another identity? Was it that I believed the Irish are the lost tribe of Israel—Leopold Bloom, *Abie's Irish Rose*? Was it some latent Jewish self-hatred? Or was it simply the relief of knowing I could pass as Gentile?

My mother used to tell me that I looked like I'd stepped out of an Irish choir. Since I had strawberry-blond hair (she called it titian), a freckled fair face, and blue eyes, I could see that she had a point. Although the rest of my family also didn't look particularly "Jewish" (by that I mean the stereotypical olive-skinned, dark-eyed, curly-haired, and hook-nosed look), they appeared different enough from me that my older brother, who never tired of inventing new ways to torture me, liked to tell me that I was adopted or, worse, fished out of the gutter by my parents, who'd felt sorry for me.

I grew up in the 1960s and '70s in Tenafly, New Jersey, a suburb of New York City. The town had four elementary-school districts. Mine, Smith, consisted mainly of nouveau riche, primarily Jewish families who lived in ugly split-levels and ranch houses on the town's eastern hill. My best friend at Smith, Suzanne, lived at the bottom of the hill, near the train tracks. Suzanne was Catholic and had nine siblings. I often went along with her to the Sunday spaghetti dinners at her church. I always felt a little guilty about being there—for both betraying my faith and trespassing on hers, but my mother would tell me it was fine.

Tenafly's four elementary schools fed into one junior high school and when I got there three of the new friends I made were, like Suzanne, good Christian churchgoing girls. They all lived on the town's north hill, in stately brick Tudor houses, the oldest in the town. Like me, they loved acting, and dancing to show tunes. Amy had the same number of siblings that Suzanne did, nine—surprising, given that she was Protestant. Her family took wildly expensive vacations.

Her father and my father were both doctors, but unlike the Bloomingdale's antique knockoffs in my house, her family's furniture was shabby and threadbare, and they drove a beat-up Volvo. And they belonged to a country club. A club that did not accept Jews as members. Jews could come as guests, though, and Amy would bring me along with her to swim. It made me a little queasy with conflict, but the country club was a lot nicer than the public pool. I suspect that, unlike the spaghetti dinners, my swimming in that pool did bother my mother. But, like so many Jewish mothers, indeed like so many mothers of all kinds, what could she do but indulge her child and let me go.

Once, when I was seventeen and my parents were away on vacation, I decided to throw a party. Word got out: open house at Susan Golomb's place. The house got overrun with teenagers while a hippie boy asked me to "mellow out" on the roof of his car. As we were doing so, suddenly the house pitched into complete darkness. It turned out that kids from Tenafly's blue-collar west side, literally the other side of the tracks, had pulled the fuses, stolen the stereo equipment, and finally, before the cops came, painted a swastika in large, thick black strokes on the front door.

A couple of months later, I went to a party thrown by a Jewish boy when a kid named John, who was as blond and blue-eyed as a Hitler Youth, started loudly making anti-Semitic remarks. My friend Lori, who was Jewish, yelled at him, "Do you know whose house you're in?" She made John back down, and I was in awe of her bravery. Still traumatized by the desecration of my home, I had just stood paralyzed, ashamed by my own silence.

I had another friend, Janet Lipsky, whose parents were both Holocaust survivors. Her father had led two escapes from concentration camps; her mother, along with her twin sister, was one of "Mengele's Children," experimented on in horrific ways. The two survivors had met in America and attained the Dream, settling in Tenafly's upper-middle-class East Hill and raising a brilliant son and daughter. But when Janet and I were in high school, her mother hanged herself. Four years later, on the anniversary of her death, Janet's brother also killed himself. For all the running, her family couldn't outrun the horror of its Jewish ancestry.

After I left home, no doubt because of my "non-Jewish" looks, people often said anti-Semitic things straight to my face. How someone was being "Jewed down" in price. How "they" all stuck together; how "they" controlled the media, the banks, hell, the world. One time, after I'd become a literary agent, I went out west to California to stay with a writer who'd sent me an early, promising draft of a novel. She told me the Russian River was getting ruined by all the Jews moving in. I told her

I was Jewish. There was an awkward silence. When the revised novel came in several months later, I didn't think her revisions were good. If they had been good, would I have represented her book? Was it because of what she'd said that I thought the revisions were poor?

Before I married and now that I'm divorced, there was always the question of when to bring up my Jewish background. One New Year's Eve I danced the night away with a man I'd just met. As we took a break to catch our breath, we got to know each other a little bit. We were both rock climbers and the children of doctors. At one point, I don't know how we got on the subject, he started to patiently tell me that on Yom Kippur the Jewish people would go down to the river to put notes of atonement on small pieces of paper and watch them sail away. I wasn't sure whether to acknowledge that this too we had in common. After all, had he been attracted to me because he thought I wasn't Jewish? On initial dates with non-Jewish men when I would feel the conversation drifting toward the subject of Israel or Judaism I preemptively mention that I'm Jewish. I do it to head off any anti-Semitic remark that might be coming my way. I realize that this amounts to a kind of prejudice itself, even if I can rationalize it as self-defense. And then if the man doesn't call me, will the reason have been that I'm Jewish? (I always toss that explanation in with all the other "never knows," like maybe I said too much, or too little, was too smart, or too dumb, my hair was the wrong color, and, of course, every woman's old saw, I was too fat.)

Once, when I was starting to date the man who did become my husband, we were out walking with a good friend of his. Out of the blue, the friend asked me, "Are you Jewish?" I glanced at my new boyfriend and saw that the color had drained from his face. Was it the boorishness of his friend's question? Or was he shocked that I could be Jewish? He was from Wisconsin—maybe he had never seen a Jew? I later learned, to my relief and delight, he had dated an Israeli before me. I made some lame joke about my curly hair covering up my horns, and the subject didn't come up between my boyfriend and me again till we were making wedding plans.

My college boyfriend was Jewish and liked to say I was a Jewish man's dream: Jewish, but I looked like a shiksa. Be forewarned: there are many among us who intentionally or not pass. Some of us, like Lauren Bacall, Scarlett Johansson, and Gwyneth Paltrow, are famous and beautiful. Each of us, I'm sure, has heard her share of anti-Semitic remarks. We toughen up. Some are pistols. My friend Lisa, in college, went out with a man named Flanders Lakewood. In a moment of drunken pique he yelled at her, "You slut, you whore, you Jew!" We couldn't stop laughing at that one. But some of the insults were devastating. A black-humored man whom I lived with for many years texted me, during the ugliest stretch of our breakup, "When they come, I will be the first to point you out."

Now I have a son. Like me, he has strawberry-blond hair and a splash of freckles across his face. When the Hasidim come around during the High Holy Days and ask, "Are you Jewish?" I always want him to say yes, to never deny his Judaism, whatever the pain it can bring. Though I had a fairly secular upbringing, my family was always culturally Jewish. I'm proud of my ancestors, who came here from the shtetls of Europe with no money, who didn't Anglicize their names, who juggled their loyalty to their heritage with their desire to assimilate.

In 1946 my father's family was showcased, in a special issue of the *Saturday Evening Post* called "Your Neighbors," as the token Jewish family. My grandfather, the son of a tailor, immigrated from Latvia as a child. He went on to found the Everlast Sporting Goods Company, a Jewish immigrant who created an

American icon. (Muhammad Ali's Everlast gloves are enshrined in the Smithsonian Museum in Washington, DC.) But I wasn't bat mitzvahed and have rarely set foot in a synagogue.

So, when my son, who is also being raised secular and has an atheist Irish Catholic father, asked to be bar mitzvahed last year I was surprised. Only a handful of his classmates are Jewish, but to him there's something compelling about being a Jew. When I asked him the reason, he said it was the tradition. He won't be of age for the ceremony for a while, and it would require that he learn Hebrew, something I doubt he'll prefer to playing video games when the time comes. But when my rabbi cousin, by way of introducing him formally to Judaism, brought him to his temple and took the Torah scrolls out of the Ark and carried them to the lectern, and then put a prayer shawl over my son and a yarmulke on his head, tears welled in my eyes. I rooted frantically in my bag for my cell phone, so that I could take a picture and send it off to my father to capture the moment before it was gone. It might be all we'll ever have if Jake decides that this was just a short role and not to be part of his identity when he becomes a man.

I wouldn't blame him if that were his decision. As I write this, on the eve of the inauguration of Donald Trump as the forty-fifth president of the United States, hate crimes have sky-rocketed nationally; in New York City, where I now live, there has been a 110 percent spike in such crimes, with Jews being the most targeted. Not only is anti-Semitism on the rise again in Europe, but on January 9, *The New York Times* reported bomb threats being made to synagogues and Jewish community centers across the East Coast of the United States. One was actually made to the center in Tenafly, where my father still lives. What was once a private concern that I only had because I heard it said enough to my face has become publicly somewhat all too easy to believe—that the worst could happen here, too. Perhaps it's already on its way.

So I am grateful to the God I'm not sure I believe in that my son does not look Jewish. After all, I am a Jewish mother.

All names in this essay, except that of the author and her immediate family, have been changed for the privacy of individuals.

Passing Ambition

/ *Sergio Troncoso* /

For the first two years of college, I passed as a Harvard student and felt more like an imposter from rural Texas who still called his *abuelita* in El Paso every Sunday, who waited for the half-crushed Express Mail box of *flautas* from his mother every few weeks, who took advantage of discovering he was an exotic Chicano—in the eyes of Radcliffe women and their visiting girl-friends—to finally get lucky in the Ivy League. Yes, I had arrived shell-shocked in Harvard Square, having never visited the school or the state, without any parents shoving twenties in my pockets or helping me open a bank account or pointing to where I could wash my clothes. It was startling, too, to be informed I had an accent, something my confident dorm mates in Hollis Hall often mentioned. When you find yourself in an alien world of your choosing, when you strive for an identity you think you want yet know little about, you become that identity on the fly, in a mix of imagination and pretense, adopting practices and knowledge on the go, trying not to lose who you are. Little did I know that pass-ing as a Harvard student would also lead to passing as a young white man in Washington, DC, during the summer of 1981.

I had not forgotten what Mr. Rodriguez from Ysleta High School had said to me when I told him I wanted to apply to JFK's alma mater, this bucolic abstraction in a printed catalog handed to me by Irma Sanchez, my high school guidance counselor, who had always had more hope for me. Mr. Rodriguez: "They don't take kids like you at Harvard." His mouth formed into a Cheshire cat smile, but it was really a smirk, with the all-knowing power of his petty position, student activities director. His face was deeply pockmarked like a brown moon, and for that I had always been grateful to the gods.

But now I was indeed at Harvard; I had survived freshman year and even scored an A minus in Expository Writing. Sophomore year I had found my academic niche—to focus on Latin America and Mexico and learn about the heritage I had not been taught in Texas schools, to take as many courses with Terry Karl and John Womack as possible. I worked for other As in their classes—miracle of miracles!—in nooks at dreary Lamont Library, walking home at midnight in the footsteps of Emerson and Thoreau. I had begun to stop passing for a Harvard student, I started believing in myself, and maybe I thought I did belong there after all. I measured and remeasured my shaky self in a process started in El Paso and continued in Cambridge: I imagined what I could be, what I wanted to be, even if I had no "right" to attain that self, even if I knew only scant details about my goal, and I would work to reach for another ledge of that self-evolution. So if passing was not being who I was at the moment, passing was also a persona I adopted when I was not satisfied, when I found I was in prickly situations I had pushed myself into prematurely, even accidentally.

That spring semester of sophomore year in 1981, I swelled again with ambition. That was my primordial mistake. At the end of freshman year, I had returned to El Paso as a stockboy to rearrange boys' T-shirts and underwear at the downtown J. C.

Penney, but now as a Harvard sophomore I set my sights higher than that bargain basement: I would try for a summer job in Washington, DC, like the other aggressive, überconfident gov jocks in Quincy House. Charles Lane, Mary Ellen Myers, Jamie Raskin, Nancy Gardner, Colin Leis, you were my heroes! I didn't want to pass as a Harvard student anymore, I wanted to *be* like these friends, and *go* where they were going. It was DC or bust for me.

Like the enterprising Harvard student I was trying to be, I started by typing letters to my congressman, Richard C. White of El Paso. A Blue Dog Democrat. A decent guy. He would help me get a job. I mailed letters to his El Paso office. (No e-mail in the Reagan years.) I mailed letters to his DC office. I wrote that I was a Harvard student, a *real* Harvard student, for goodness' sake! Wouldn't it be great to employ me in his office? I would do anything! I was a gov major—and bilingual! I included my résumé. I waited for the congressman's response. Nothing for weeks. I would make this happen, one way or another. I mailed more letters to White, to my senators. Still nothing. It was March of 1981. I was nervous. Summer was just two months away. I wasn't going back to J. C. Penney. I needed to earn spending money for college that summer, but I wasn't going back to ripping up box after box of Fruit of the Loom whities and lugging the merchandise in dirty-ass pushcarts, even if the hottest young *mexicanas* from El Paso and Juárez, in the tightest of dresses, were also selling our wares in that dingy basement.

One day I discovered the housing board at the JFK School of Government and noticed that enticing opportunities from alumni were posted for current Harvard/Radcliffe students searching for summer housing in DC. One pink index card was from a Margo Stever, who lived in Chevy Chase, Maryland, and in exchange for sitting for her toddler and doing a few extra chores at their house—her husband was a lawyer—the enterprising student could have a place to stay and even use of a car! I knew exactly what Colin or Jamie or Nancy or Charles or Mary Ellen would do. They would snap up this opportunity as soon as they saw it—and so did I. I called Mrs. Stever and introduced myself and lied. I told her I had a summer job working for my congressman already. I would be in Washington, DC; I could paint their fence, and yes, I knew how to paint a room too, since I had done construction work for my father for many years. Painting had been my specialty as an *obrero* in my father's apartment buildings, and for room and board too. (I guess my father did throw love into that bargain as well, but that deal only meant he wasn't shy about working my brothers and me like *mojados*.) So Margo and I agreed to our bargain in Chevy Chase. I had no job, but I had a place to stay in DC. There was no turning back now.

April, and still not a word from Congressman White. I was desperate. Using my handy MCI calling card again, I phoned his DC office from a pay phone in Quincy House. After several tries, and "Please call back when So-and-So, the office manager, will be available," I finally reached Mrs. So-and-So. I don't remember her name. I told her I was from El Paso, Texas, I was a Harvard student (in my heart, a *real* Harvard student), and I was looking for a summer internship. Her first words crushed me: Congressman Richard C. White's office had already awarded their two summer internships earlier this year, in February, to students from the University of Texas at Austin and Southern Methodist University. No more internships were to be had from his office.

Mrs. So-and-So was pleasant-sounding enough, but pleasant in that deadly way a steel magnolia would be, with that Southern twang just driving it sweetly (and subtly) home that even a Chicano from Harvard was still a Chicano, and not a blond rich kid whose parents had connections with White, and not the progeny of a donor contributing thousands of dollars to multiple reelection campaigns, certainly not the son of a good ol' boy who regularly played golf with White at the Coronado Country Club. Or so I imagined. In trying to be who you are not quite yet, you fight so many real and imagined demons in your mind, from the voices of self-racism in your own community to those very real voices intending to exclude you subtly as well as by slamming a door in your face. You fight what you don't know and what you should have known, had you been in the know. Chicano shadowboxing. I had been defeated before I had even plunged into this quest for DC and official gov jock status: by the time I applied and sent my queries, all the internships had already been handed out. I hated myself for not knowing the rules, for not even knowing the right deadlines, for my parents who didn't play golf (even though they adored Lee Treviño and all his Merry Mexicanness), and for everything and nothing in that beer-splashed Quincy House phone booth.

Then I did something rash: I declared to Mrs. So-and-So that I had already committed to summer housing in DC, that I could not turn back, that I was going to DC this summer one way or another. I may have even thrown in a line about also being a voter in El Paso (absentee ballot), and how Congressman White should be helping all of the constituents in his district. My tone certainly hinted "troublemaker," whether I intended it or not. I was desperate, I tell you. I had nothing to lose. This stubbornness had come from my hardscrabble life in Ysleta (*el terco*, they always jeered at me), but my bullheadedness had also been refined (sublimated, if you will) at Harvard into sharp words and phrases and a putting-yourself-out-there semiconfidence, with a dash of the kamikaze too. To my great surprise, Mrs. So-and-So softened, welcomed me to visit her office when I arrived in Washington, and even added, "We will find you something; don't you worry."

I was over the moon! I was a real Harvard student! No more pretending to be a gov jock at Quincy House with my impressive colleagues. I would be like them. I would be *with* them: a Harvard summer intern in Washington, DC! I had taken another step beyond passing, from existing uneasily as an outsider at Harvard without a clue, to being a successful government major at Harvard. I had leaped from vaguely dreaming to be what I didn't know much about, to achieving specifically one part of what I thought I wanted. I blurted out the news of my summer internship to Colin Leis, my best real friend in that group, as he walked by the pinball machines at Quincy. He congratulated me. I treated myself to an Elsie burger at Elsie's on Mt. Auburn Street, my favorite way to celebrate anything good that happened to me in or around Harvard Square, where Chicanos from El Paso were as rare as true-believing, trickle-down Reaganauts.

I arrived in DC in June, after my final exams, after I had sent a letter to White's office confirming my conversation with Mrs. So-and-So, the office manager. I had not heard anything back. My serape from Juárez, Technics speakers and stereo from J. C. Penney, the Sunbeam electric frying pan heirloom (circa 1957) my mother had bestowed upon me to reheat her *flautas*, dozens of books on Latin America's political economy and oil politics, the class notes for my first two years at Harvard—all of this stuff was already in boxes in the basement of Old Quincy. I was ready for a new start this summer. I took a taxi from National Airport to Chevy Chase, Maryland, which seemed so green, suburban, and orderly it was a shock to my eyes. Raymond Street was that perfect street I had always imagined in Charlie Brown specials, always somewhere *over there*, eons from the US-Mexico border of dusty Ysleta and El Paso, somewhere in the Valhalla of the Northeast where everyone carved pumpkins on their porches on Halloween and jumped into piles of brown, red, yellow leaves and hugged loser, big-headed boys who couldn't pitch worth a damn. The Stevers even had a white picket fence in front of their yard. I would be painting that white picket fence all summer.

I arrived on a Friday and would start work on Monday. Margo was a hippie poet from the 1960s with a blond toddler named David. She was sweet and shrill at the same time, always looking after my well-being with a squeaky voice that sometimes reminded me of a cartoon mouse and at other times of nails raked across a chalkboard. I noted the Swedish cereal we had for breakfast the first morning, the framed Japanese prints handed down from previous generations, and the maroon Volvo in the driveway. That summer I would also meet the poet Denise Levertov, Margo's best friend. The incongruities were what confused me: extremely progressive politics and a toddler-friendly, even messy household, yet unmistakable signs of wealth, power, and high culture.

Don Stever was an environmental lawyer who worked for the Justice Department, with a deep interest in literature and music. That first weekend at the Stevers, they invited me to a barbecue at a neighbor's home—we were surrounded by Washington lawyers and lobbyists in tony Chevy Chase—and Don and his bluegrass band entertained the gathering with Grateful Dead songs, Don plucking his bass, his face so concentrated, his musicianship astonishing to me. In my twenty-year-old mind, Don and Margo were beings from another planet who were experts at such disparate crafts. As soon as I thought I knew who they were, they would surprise me. They were fascinated by Latin American politics, the Sandinistas' overthrow of Somoza in Nicaragua, the violence in El Salvador, the United States' history of murderous colonialism, and the certain subterfuge of the Reagan administration.

I remember at that first barbecue in Chevy Chase feeling like both an outsider and an idiot in a blue blazer, while these savvy and confident lawyers wore jeans and rolled up the sleeves of their button-down shirts. Some tried their Spanish on me, and I had a certain cred because of it, because I was a *mexicano* from El

Paso at Harvard. Yet it was a mask I donned in order to survive, and I knew it was a mask, a mask that would play well with this friendly, liberal crowd. They put me in a certain box I would come to know—the scholarship boy, the poor Harvard Chicano, the pet project—and I let them, because I didn't know who I was, because I was scrambling at every minute of every day in Chevy Chase. Whenever you pass as someone other than who you are, the presumption is that you know who you are first of all, and then you decide *not* to be that. I didn't know anything. I certainly didn't know who I was, and I could only guess at who I wanted to be. I just wanted to survive this Washington wonderland thrust upon me by my ambition.

In that maroon Volvo, Don drove me to my first day in the Cannon House Office Building on Capitol Hill. I was so excited, and Don told me to meet him at the Justice Department whenever I was done with my workday. That would be our routine. As I walked up the steps to the main entrance at Cannon, I was whistling Vivaldi's *Four Seasons*; the "Spring" allegro was the only classical music I knew. I had started listening to NPR in Chevy Chase every morning.

Instructed by the front guards, I searched the halls of Cannon for Representative White's office. Striding by me on both sides of the wide, yellow hallways were other young people sharply attired, many blond and brunette, certainly many good-looking, even the men, who reminded me of quarterbacks from Coronado High School in El Paso, and the women their cheerleaders. Okay, some of the men did look like fat quarterbacks a decade or so after high school and college frat parties. In a hurry, everyone knew exactly where they were going; I didn't. I found Richard C. White's office and got ready for my Washington adventure.

After sitting for a few minutes in what seemed to me posh, velvety chairs, I was led into the office of Mrs. So-and-So, which wasn't really an office but a series of cubicles (she had the biggest one). Behind the cubicles were two large, forbidding oak doors, which presumably opened to the congressman's lair. Everyone seemed speeded up in that office, answering phones, or interrupting with questions, or walking past you as if you did not exist. Mrs. So-and-So sized me up and asked me where I was from in El Paso and smiled in that sweet and deadly way, as if a knife were about to be pushed into your gut, but nicely: "*Sir*-gee-oh, that's raight, isn't it? Y'all be in the mailroom. Feell these forms out, honey, and I'll take you thaire in just a sec."

The Cannon Office mailroom was in the basement, or maybe even the subbasement, and where I was to work was this hothouse of elongated, cacophonous machines, dozens of them. These old-world printers and folders gushed out hundreds, nay thousands, of flyers and circulars every congressman mails you, which you rip up in disgust along with every other piece of junk mail. This was the dark and doomed epicenter of the useless Capitol Hill propaganda that details what little the men and women of Congress have accomplished and how many photo ops they can show you to trick you into thinking otherwise. Every sweaty worker in that subterranean half-haze was wearing a T-shirt, many in wife beaters. I was the only "white guy" in that basement, and the black workers at the first machines stared at me as if I were this odd duck dropped into their pond. Remember that scene in *Rocky III* when Rocky goes into Apollo Creed's LA gym, with the leaky pipes, and the sweat heavy in the air, and every muscled black boxer wanting to rip Rocky's heart out? Well, it was like that, but worse. I was no Rocky Balboa in a blue blazer.

As my mind reeled as to why White's office had stranded me there and how this was not what I had imagined my summer internship to be, I was instructed by the floor manager and directed to one machine, to the end of it, to stack the folded flyers spewing out of its clackety metal mouth into boxes. For now, that would be my job. Before noon, I was sweating so heavily I had taken off my blue blazer and tie and rolled them into a ball. The African American workers did not talk to me at first, and only glared and told me what to do: here I was passing as a white guy dumped in their work area, a clueless idiot. I was scared half out of my mind, because I didn't know how to work the machinery, because I didn't know why I was there, and because I hadn't imagined I would be going back to life as an *obrero* worse than the J. C. Penney's basement. I just wanted to survive, so I said nothing and worked and passed for the "white orphan" in the Cannon basement. That first day I had forgotten to bring any lunch—I just thought I could go buy it somewhere quickly—and our work rules meant we had less than an hour for lunch, to get to lunch and to actually eat it. "Work rules" meant I had joined the union, which indeed I had when I filled out my paperwork. In retrospect, joining the union was the best thing that ever happened to me that summer: I was able to earn more money in one month than I had in three at the J. C. Penney in El Paso.

The first person to talk to me, other than to bark orders or warnings, was Freddy. I don't remember his last name. He was this skinny, semi-shy African American in a thick T-shirt. He never wore the wife beaters, nor the gauzy, thin T-shirts, and he was always modest about his appearance. He reminded me of a lightweight boxer, with long muscles in his forearms and the tightest of stomachs. Freddy offered me half his peanut butter sandwich that first day and told me to pack a lunch the next day. I know he felt sorry for me, and frankly I was glad that he did, because I was hungry. Passing for a pathetic white guy had that small advantage in the basement. Freddy also mentioned I could go upstairs into the cafeteria at Cannon, but I imagined all the other "real interns" would be there, the beautiful people I had seen in the hallways, and I didn't want to show up sweat-stained, disheveled, defeated. That first week, I would bring extra apples and oranges with my lunch from the Stevers, for Freddy. After I had felt I had repaid him for his kindness that first day, I would trade food with Freddy for whatever he liked that I had and whatever I wanted from his pile. That first week, Freddy also asked me, "Hey, Sergio, why the hell aren't you upstairs?" Good question. I had no answer then.

In retrospect, Mrs. So-and-So probably put me in the mailroom because she had no other place for me and wanted to avoid trouble, because she guessed correctly that I needed the money, and because I didn't pass for a powerful Harvard student from Texas (who could somehow damage White politically) but as a Chicano at Harvard, maybe too aggressive, needing to be put in his place, willing to work even if it was only shit work. As trying to be who you want to be (but are not), passing is as much dependent on the agent-self making an effort as it is on what *others* think of you, what others allow you to be, in their eyes, perceptions you might be trying to change, root and branch. For that beleaguered agent-self, the point is to never give up.

I lied to Don and Margo every day of that summer while I was in the basement of the Cannon House Office Building. I would clean myself after work every day, in a bathroom I found that was often empty. I would smooth out my blazer and tie before I climbed into the Volvo at the Justice Department for the ride home. I would make up stories about what I did in White's office: answering constituent mail, attending hearings for the congressman and writing notes, rewriting policy papers. All of these stories I overheard from my Harvard/Radcliffe gov-jock friends I saw on the weekends at Georgetown parties. Their summer internships were fabulous. These summer interns hobnobbed with senators and diplomats and whispered about juicy sexcapades. I was having none of that. I was passing for a real summer intern with the Stevers and my college friends; I was passing for a white guy in the Cannon basement; I was passing for a real Harvard student with all of them.

The floor manager in the Cannon basement designated me to deliver the boxes of flyers and other propaganda crap to the offices upstairs, and so on many Thursdays and Fridays I pushed a cart through the halls of Cannon, a sweaty worker from the bowels of Congress invading again the territory of the elite, the important, and the higher class. I would think about how everyone in the basement (except me) was black, and how everyone upstairs in the hallways and offices of Cannon was white, too often blond, and often female—gorgeous Southern belles who eagerly trailed the often-male members of Congress or their male political chiefs. The disparities were stark. Right before my eyes, in the halls of Congress, the inequalities, prejudices, and lecheries of our country were in full display for anyone who cared to look. Whenever I saw someone who was African American in a suit and tie and displaying that confident, aggressive walk of someone in power, or close to power, or a similar someone who might be Latino, it was like spotting a black unicorn in the hallways.

After I had worked one month in the basement and nagged Congressman White's office about internships anywhere else on Capitol Hill, Mrs. So-and-So asked to see me. She told me they had found me an unpaid internship at the Congressional Sunbelt Council, for my last six weeks of the summer. This was what I had been waiting for. I didn't like not getting paid, but I had made so much money as a union worker that first month that I didn't need to save more money for college that summer. For my last week, when the floor manager was out of sight, Freddy showed me how to operate one of the massive machines—pulling this lever and cranking that handle to produce the perfect flyer.

John Buchanan, a former rep from Alabama, was the executive director of the Sunbelt Council, but the real power behind the throne—and an affable, even honest politico—was George Kassouf, this young lawyer with wild curly black hair. He taught me to be cynical, but in a friendly way, to look at Washington for what it really was, and to not lose my soul in these halls of Congress. George, for some reason, enjoyed having these philosophical discussions with me, and he knew about the segregation between the basement workers and the people in power upstairs. He taught me to understand how the District of Columbia was kind of a colony of Congress. I'm not sure much has changed since those days.

What I remember most about my experience at the Sunbelt Council was how much I hated it, how boring it was, and how I regretted getting what I had strived for in a way. Except for my lunches with George Kassouf, I thought it was a waste of time. All we did was curry favor for the congressional members of the Sunbelt Council, create studies to prove preordained conclusions, and write worthless reports supporting tepid political views that did not alienate any House members from the southern and southwestern states. It was all about politics, and politics had nothing to do with what was best for the country, or what was right: it had to do with power, and who could hurt you if you crossed them, and whether you could hurt them more in retaliation, if necessary.

I had become a "real" gov jock at the end of that summer of 1981, the only kind of "real Harvard student" I felt I could achieve, by passing as that kind of student when I had no idea what that meant, by passing as a summer intern and white guy in the Cannon basement when I wasn't. More importantly, I had learned that ambition could be my worst enemy. When I got what I wanted—what I imagined I wanted—I saw how meaningless politics and this political world were. Why had I fought to be a real gov jock at Harvard? That's the question I couldn't stop thinking about as I returned to school. I carried that question with me as I delved deeper into history and philosophy in my coursework. When I started writing stories about the border to give voice to characters from my home, when I melded those

stories with philosophical and psychological questions I had refined in school, then I found meaning in my work, literary work.
Something that was mine, uniquely mine, authentically mine.
I wasn't passing as anything anymore. I felt I finally was who I
wanted to be by doing the work of creative observation that is
storytelling, that is philosophy in literature, that is being a voice
for outsiders who had no voice.

To pass as who you are not requires imagination and ambition; to reach what you are not requires guile and grit and even
luck; to *know* what you want, the hardest of this tripartition, is
a recursive process of trying and passing and attaining, and then
thinking about the plateau you have reached. What I learned is
that even if you reach the goal you want—the self you want—you
still have to interrogate yourself if that goal is a worthy one, if the
self you have achieved is what you thought it would be before you
achieved it. If it isn't, then you need to give yourself the space and
time to work out who you want to be. You always owe yourself
that self-respect.

Terror and Passing

/ Rafia Zakaria /

In the fall of 2016 I was to fly to Denver for the launch of a paper at the Online News Association's annual conference. As a Muslim American, I have a standard protocol that I follow prior to and during air travel. I stay away from the brightly colored tunics that I usually wear, I wear more makeup than usual, and I smile a lot whether or not I have any reason to. I fret over whether my jewelry, the pendant with *Allah* written in Arabic, the silver scroll necklace that contains a prayer, can be taken along.

Sometimes I leave them behind (my purse could be searched and they could be found). At other times, when I have the luxury of a checked bag, I take them along, secreted in rolls of clothing. I have been told that TSA agents are trained to look out for these distinctive giveaways so that they know to pull Muslims out of the line, mark them for further checking.

It is not just how I appear that I worry over; there is also the issue of what I carry with me and what I carry it in. A tote bag that has Urdu* lettering and in which I usually carry my computer is a

---

* Urdu, the language of my native Pakistan.

no. The keyboard overlay with Urdu letters that I use if I want to type in Urdu is also a no. I go through the call and message log on my cell phone and erase all the text messages that are in Urdu. I ponder over whether I should delete all the text messages from people with Arabic names, even when they are written in English, and keep only the ones with safe American names. I wonder if I should give safe American code names to all my family and all the friends who don't have them. I have a bad memory and so I do not do this, plus having a code may appear incriminating just in itself.

On this day and this flight to Denver, there is an additional conundrum. I have been reading Joby Warrick's book *Black Flags: The Rise of ISIS* and am about a hundred pages in. I want to use the hours of waiting at the airport and on the flight and at the many other junctures of travel that require it, to get further into the book. I write about terrorism, the paper I am presenting is about terrorism, so it makes sense to read this book.

At the same time, I know that it is a risk. As an American Muslim I cannot be reading a book about terrorism on an airplane. I have friends and colleagues who have been pulled off planes for far less, for reading books about Syria, for watching soap operas in Urdu, for listening to Arabic music, and even just for saying *inshallah* (God willing) as they hang up their cell phone. The book in my hands on an airplane is a provocation in an America whose fear has made it rabid, where all Muslims are only terrorists, never doctors or lawyers or even journalists. Where truth is not tolerated, trickery must intervene. I look through my bookshelf, then proceed to exchange the dust cover of the Warrick book with that of another hardback. *The Rise of ISIS* accompanies me in drag, dressed now as *Georgia,* Dawn Tripp's novel on the life of the artist Georgia O'Keeffe.

— — —

I get through security that day without event. If the calculations of wins and losses were simple, my passing through would be a triumph. I had navigated the narrow bridge over the river of fire that the security checkpoint is for America's Muslims. The truth, of course, is complicated, not so easily enclosed within a single metaphor. Altering one's appearance is an abridgement of the self. Subterfuge based on changing all that is visible, all that *can* be changed, feels because of this inherently subversive. An enormous chunk of identity we know comes via ascriptions, the constantly present judgments of others. It is no surprise, then, that even when I do make it through security, based on the sum of all my machinations I feel no relief but rather shame. To have succeeded in hiding something that should not need to have been hidden at all is no success at all.

Poised at the post-checkpoint moment, I wonder if I should confess that I am Muslim, that the book is really about ISIS, that there's been a mistake in letting me through. All the effort at passing has left me with a scabrous sore, it itches and instinctively I want to scratch, even bleed. I feel angry and resentful that my potential as a terrorist is being judged and gauged by others who know nothing about me. Within this scheme of evaluation and judgment operative at America's airports there is no room for the truth I know about myself, that I am not and never will be a terrorist.

I have reasons for fear that go beyond being checked at airport security. In the days and weeks prior I have been immersed in research related to the prosecution of ISIS terrorists in the United States. My bafflement and alarm at the scant proof and zealous prosecutions I have read about has left me playing a perverse game with myself. Per its prescriptions I imagine I am the FBI and develop a case against myself under the US statute outlawing material support for terrorism.

Unlike nearly all other criminal statutes in the United States, this one, whose words and provisions I have read over and over again, criminalizes not a criminal act, or even the intent of a criminal act, but simply anything or something that can be interpreted as possibly supporting terrorism. "Terrorism," the legal term, can in turn only be applied to the actions of a "foreign" group. I know that the prosecutions the material support law has yielded are terrifyingly incidental; in one case, trips to visit family in a Muslim country have qualified as "connection or collaboration with a foreign terrorist organization," and in another, posting on a website that is frequented by some belonging to extremist groups has been enough to yield a conviction and a decades-long sentence. A poetess who submitted a poem to a man who went on to edit the al-Qaeda magazine and who also checked out a chemistry book from the library awaits trial in Brooklyn. A disaffected sixteen-year-old posting about the transfer of funds via Bitcoin from his mother's basement in Virginia has been tried and convicted. In all the cases, what the defendants *said* about themselves or their intentions is irrelevant; it is some unseen process of radicalization imagined as being underway by their accusers that is determinative. A random set of visible factors is deemed incontrovertible evidence pointing to this invisible process, a potentiality that justifies punitive measures, despite its own unreality.

In the macabre game I play in my own head, I wonder how close I come to being one of this sorry group, and I put together the random facts that could be assembled for my own prosecution. I have taken several trips to Pakistan and even one to Turkey, both countries where terrorist activity takes place. I have on numerous occasions downloaded jihadist propaganda (would it matter that I opposed it, had to write about it?). I have at one time or another interviewed people who may know people who have had extremist sympathies. Then there is social media, the basis of more than 80 percent of the actual prosecutions under the statute. Here too I could be made to appear culpable; I have a number of Facebook friends and Twitter followers whose true identities I do not know, who could know jihadists or even be jihadists. To top it all off I sometimes conclude, as I build the case against myself, my careful efforts at passing, the fake file names, the secreted necklaces and unacknowledged proficiency in Urdu, can all be construed as the wrong kind of deceptions, the sort that portend the very worst.

At the conference in Denver I do a show-and-tell. I hold up my book and peel back the floral cover of *Georgia* to reveal what I have really been reading. I know that my audience of journalists cannot imagine themselves being thrown off a plane, let alone prosecuted, for made-up terror crimes. I tell them that while I am a journalist to them, justified hence in my curiosity about ISIS or my downloads of jihadist propaganda, that reality does not extend into the world on the other side of the hotel's glass walls. Beyond those, at airport security, on the street and in the eyes of law enforcement, I am just another Muslim in America, lacking specificity, part of a suspicious mass of potential terror that must be policed and profiled and, if at all possible, preemptively imprisoned.

It is a reality from which I cannot escape and a perverse contest that I cannot win. Looking too much like a terrorist makes me suspect and looking too little like a terrorist also makes me suspect. After all, the FBI could say, wouldn't ISIS select someone who can pass, appear unthreateningly innocent, as the perfect operative, as their ideal operative?

— — —

What is insufficiently American, too alarmingly Muslim, at the airports of one part of the world, is inadequately Muslim and too terrifyingly American at others. In February of 2011 I was traveling as I often do to Karachi, Pakistan. The routes for travel between Pakistan and the United States require a stop in either Europe or one of the Gulf States. On this journey, I had chosen to stop in Abu Dhabi, in the United Arab Emirates; the tickets on Gulf carriers were cheaper than those of the European ones and it felt good to have more than half of the twenty-four-hour-plus journey over and done with by the time I disembarked.

During the layover in Abu Dhabi, I did what I always do on my way to Pakistan. I went into a restroom and changed out of the yoga pants and T-shirt that I had worn to pass security and suspicion at American airports and into the *shalwar kameez* (long tunic and loose pants) that would make it easier to pass through the airport where I was headed. Around my new outfit I wrapped a soft shawl that covered nearly all of my body. I thought I was ready for Karachi.

In the few weeks prior to my arrival, a shocking event had taken place on the streets of Pakistan. A man named Raymond Davis, a CIA contractor, had killed two men while driving through the city of Lahore. Then a diplomatic vehicle on its way to rescue Davis had killed a third man. The circumstances related to why he had killed the men (or why the third man was run over) were unclear. It was known that the US government had invoked diplomatic immunity (even though Davis was not technically a diplomat) as a defense, asking that Davis be released from the custody of Pakistani police immediately. The diplomatic wrangling between the United States and Pakistan had been underway for weeks, hogging the headlines and breaking-news bulletins, even on the day I landed in Karachi.

Dressed in traditional clothes, I walked through the airport to passport control. There are several lines demarcated for this purpose at the Karachi airport. Since flights from the West normally arrive in the middle of the night or in the early-morning hours, there is usually only one line that is actually staffed. All passport holders, Pakistani or otherwise, queue up, save those who have connections in high places. They do not have to stand in line at all.

Groggy and exhausted, I was standing in the one general line when a male immigration official approached me: "Are you traveling by yourself?" he asked. When I answered yes, he asked me to step aside and toward another counter off to the side. I worried as I did this; being asked to step aside is never a good omen at airports, and it is a particularly problematic one at the Karachi airport, where it is difficult to tell between an official looking for a bribe and one actually wielding authority. Unsure, I followed him mutely to the separate counter where he led me. Standing behind it, with my American passport before him, he began asking me a series of questions. What was the purpose of my visit to Pakistan? Who exactly were the relatives I would be visiting? Why did I travel so frequently between the United States and Pakistan? Had I ever worked for a US government agency? My heart raced as I answered the man's questions. I had traveled between the countries scores of times and never before had I met such treatment. I wondered if I should stop talking, make a fuss, demand to speak to a superior.

In the meantime, the man's questions became even more vexing. Finally, putting the tips of his fingers together and looking directly at me, he asked, "Have you ever intended to harm the interests or security of Pakistan?" I looked up at him, something I had avoided doing until now, and answered with a firm no. Women from good families never look directly at any men, I had been taught, and I knew the rule applied in Pakistan. Until that moment, I believed that the best course of action was to pretend that I was just another Pakistani American housewife, visiting the homeland alone to tend to a sick parent (the second part was true). With this last question, I realized that he was implying that I, like the jailed Raymond Davis, was an American spy.

I may have been dressed like a Pakistani, have been speaking Urdu without an accent, have effected the correct body language of a woman in a male-dominated society, but I was not in the eyes of this official "passing." In that moment I felt closer than I had ever been until then to "disappearing," a term used to describe being spirited away by Pakistan's intelligence agencies. I was surprised when he let me go.

I met my family outside the airport but said nothing of what had happened; it would be of no use, I told myself. They would be scared, worry endlessly of what I would face on my way back.

The terrifying thing about encounters such as these is that it is difficult to capture the terror of their occurrence. The descriptions and questions seem nondescript or perhaps even routine; it is via the mien and unmistakable malevolence of their delivery that they are able to invoke fear. I would try to dissect and reconstruct all of it in the days that followed, coming up with answers that were more clever or glib, asking for a superior, making a loud fuss such that I drew the attention of the people milling about. Harassing a woman is shameful in Pakistan, particularly if the woman starts to yell and scream. It may have ended my ordeal, enabled and facilitated my passing.

— — —

I realize that some of my conundrums as a Muslim, as an American, as a Pakistani, and as a woman are borne of an identity that exists and inhabits the margins of several separate wholes. The fraught relationships between the constituent parts of myself are fought on the terrain of my physical and visible self. What I choose to wear or not wear, what I say, the language in which I say it, the conventions I follow, the conventions I flout are all a paean of loyalty to one or another. Each side demands more than the logic of a world made up mostly of wholes requiring that I choose one and renounce the other, be only American or only Pakistani, only Muslim or only female.

There is, however, a greater, more universal truth about the act of passing that transcends the peculiarities of my own or other hyphenated conditions. The burden of passing, its central fault, lies not in its success or failure as an endeavor, but rather in the requirement of deception that it imposes on all those who engage in it. Inherent in this deception is the clear message of inadequacy, of falling short, of being less than an ideal, inferior to an original. It is this kernel of untruth demanded, of selfhood corroded, that is the burden of passing, one that weighs down the manner and mien of all those on whose shoulders it rests.

NOTES ON CONTRIBUTORS

GABRIELLE BELLOT is a staff writer for *Literary Hub*. Her work has appeared in the *Atlantic*, the *New York Times*, *Guernica*, *Slate*, *Huffington Post*, *Tin House*, *Electric Literature*, *Lambda Literary*, the blogs of *Prairie Schooner* and the *Missouri Review*, and many other places.

TREY ELLIS is a novelist, screenwriter, playwright, essayist, and associate professor at Columbia University. He is the author of the novels *Platitudes*, *Home Repairs*, and the American Book Award–winning *Right Here, Right Now*, as well as the memoir *Bedtime Stories*. His work for the screen includes the Peabody-winning and Emmy-nominated HBO film *The Tuskegee Airmen*. Ellis lives in Westport, Connecticut.

MARC FITTEN is an editor and author. He has published opinion pieces in the *New York Times*, *International Herald Tribune*, and *Atlanta Journal-Constitution*. His novels, *Valeria's Last Stand* and *Elsa's Kitchen*, have been translated into half a dozen languages. He is currently at work on his third book and spends too much time researching his family history. He lives in Atlanta.

SUSAN GOLOMB is a literary agent who lives and works in New York City.

MARGO JEFFERSON is a cultural critic and the author of the National Book Critic's Circle Award–winning *Negroland: A Memoir* and *On Michael Jackson*. She was a staff writer for the *New York Times* and received a Pulitzer Prize in 1995. Her essays have been widely published and anthologized. She teaches writing at Columbia University and lives in New York City.

M. G. LORD is the author, most recently, of *The Accidental Feminist: How Elizabeth Taylor Raised Our Consciousness and We Were Too Distracted by Her Beauty to Notice*, which won a Los Angeles Press Club award. She is also the author of *Forever Barbie: The Unauthorized Biography of a Real Doll* and *Astro Turf*, for which she was awarded an Alfred P. Sloan science-writing grant. She has written for the *New York Times Book Review*, the *Los Angeles Times*, and many other venues. She teaches at the University of Southern California and the Yale Writers' Conference, and makes her home in Los Angeles.

ACHY OBEJAS is the author of *Ruins* and *Days of Awe*, among other works. She translated, into Spanish, Junot Diaz's *The Brief Wondrous Life of Oscar Wao* and *This Is How You Lose Her*, and into English, Rita Indiana's *Papi* and Carlos Velasquez's *The Cowboy Bible*. The founder of Mills College's MFA in translation, she is also the recipient, among many awards, of a USA Ford Fellowship for her writing and translation. Her most recent book is *The Tower of the Antilles & Other Stories*. She lives in the San Francisco Bay Area.

CLARENCE PAGE, a syndicated columnist and member of the *Chicago Tribune*'s editorial board, won the 1989 Pulitzer Prize for Commentary, among his other honors. His latest book, *Culture Worrier*, a collection of his columns, was published in 2014. Page lives in Washington, DC.

LISA PAGE is a writer and instructor. Her work has appeared in the *Virginia Quarterly Review*, *American Short Fiction*, the *Crisis*, *Playboy*, *Playbill*, and the *Washington Post Book World*. She directs the creative writing program at George Washington University and teaches at the Yale Writers' Conference. She lives in Maryland, in the DC metropolitan area.

DOLEN PERKINS-VALDEZ is the author of two critically acclaimed historical novels: *Wench* and *Balm*. Her novels explore African American life before and after the Civil War. She has been a finalist for two NAACP Image Awards and the Hurston-Wright Legacy Award for fiction. *Wench* received the First Novelist Award from the Black Caucus of the American Library Association. A graduate of Harvard and a former University of California President's Postdoctoral Fellow at UCLA, she lives in Washington, DC, with her family.

PATRICK ROSAL is the author of *Brooklyn Antediluvian*, his fourth full-length collection of poetry. He is the son of Filipino immigrants from the Ilocos region of the archipelago and was born and raised in New Jersey. He lives in Philadelphia.

BRANDO SKYHORSE's debut novel, *The Madonnas of Echo Park*, received the PEN/Hemingway Award and the Sue Kaufman Prize for First Fiction from the American Academy of Arts and Letters. *Take This Man: A Memoir* was named by *Kirkus Reviews* as one of the Best Nonfiction Books of the year. Skyhorse has been awarded fellowships at Ucross Foundation and the Breadloaf Writers' Conference, and was a Jenny McKean Moore writer-in-residence at George Washington University. A graduate of Stanford University and the MFA Writers' Workshop program at the University of California, Irvine, Skyhorse is an associate professor of English at Indiana University in Bloomington.

SERGIO TRONCOSO is the author of *The Last Tortilla and Other Stories*, *Crossing Borders: Personal Essays*, and the novels *The Nature of Truth* and *From This Wicked Patch of Dust*. He co-edited *Our Lost Border: Essays on Life amid the Narco-Violence*. Among the numerous awards he has won are the Premio Aztlan Literary Prize, Southwest Book Award, Bronze Award for Essays from *ForeWord Reviews*, International Latino Book Award, and Bronze Award for Multicultural Fiction from *ForeWord Reviews*. He is a resident faculty member of the Yale Writers' Conference and an instructor at the Hudson Valley Writers' Center in Sleepy Hollow, New York. Troncoso lives in New York City.

TERESA WILTZ is a veteran journalist who has worked for the *Washington Post*, the *Chicago Tribune*, the *Root*, and *Essence*. As a staff writer on the *Chicago Tribune*'s metropolitan news desk, she was part of the reporting team that won the Robert F. Kennedy Journalism Award Grand Prize for a series on murdered children in Chicago. She is the author of *The Real America: The Tangled Roots of Race and Identity*. Wiltz lives in Washington, DC.

RAFIA ZAKARIA is a columnist for *Dawn* (Pakistan) and the *Boston Review*'s Reading Other Women series. She is the author of *The Upstairs Wife: An Intimate History of Pakistan*, which was named the best global nonfiction of 2015 by *Newsweek*. She has written for the *New York Times*, *Guardian*, *New Republic*, *Nation*, *Guernica*, and various other publications. She lives in Indianapolis.

ACKNOWLEDGMENTS

Lisa Page thanks:

For all your support, ideas, and friendship—Dini Karasik, George Pelecanos, Sunny Fischer, and Tom Mallon.

For your instruction and guidance—Susan Shreve, Maxine Clair, Carole Stovall, and Edward P. Jones.

For your love, brilliance, and inspiration—Grady Page; the late, great, Grady Johnson; Leslie Piotrowski; and Clarence Page.

Brando Skyhorse thanks:

For giving us an Origin(s) point—Dini Karasik (origins journal.com).

For your collaboration, vision, courage, and stories—Lisa Page and our fantastic contributors.

For outstanding editorial support and an inexhaustible patience that made this book possible—Gayatri Patnaik.

For making us feel like rock stars—Helene Atwan and the entire Beacon Press staff.

For encouraging me to teach what I know about passing—Sean McCann and Stephanie Weiner.

For teaching me more than I ever knew about passing—my FYE students at Wesleyan University (Spring 2016) and my Bennington College students (Fall 2016).

For family—Adriana, Kereny, Natalie, Aurora, Candido, Dillan, Marco, and John Madrid.

For giving "Team Skycat" the wings to soar and knowing *exactly* who I am—Erin Kelley.

Frank Zamora and Chris Hokanson—I miss you.